My Year of Really Bad Dates

My Year of Really Bad Dates

A Memoir

Rachel J. Lithgow

SHE WRITES PRESS

Copyright © 2025 Rachel J. Lithgow

All rights reserved. No part of this publication may be reproduced, stored in a retrieval system, or transmitted in any form or by any means, electronic, mechanical, photocopying, recording, or otherwise, except for brief quotations in reviews, educational works, or other uses permitted by copyright law.

Published in 2026 by
She Writes Press, an imprint of The Stable Book Group

32 Court Street, Suite 2109
Brooklyn, NY 11201
https://shewritespress.com

Print ISBN: 979-8-89636-010-0
E-ISBN: 979-8-89636-011-7
Library of Congress Control Number: 2025911615

Interior designer: Katherine Lloyd, The DESK

Printed in the United States

Names and identifying characteristics have been changed to protect the privacy of certain individuals.

No part of this publication may be used to train generative artificial intelligence (AI) models. The publisher and author reserve all rights related to the use of this content in machine learning.

All company and product names mentioned in this book may be trademarks or registered trademarks of their respective owners. They are used for identification purposes only and do not imply endorsement or affiliation.Names and identifying characteristics have been changed to protect the privacy of certain individuals.

For Ava and Archie
And for everyone who has been
told they aren't enough

Prologue

"THE CLINTONS HAD JEFFREY EPSTEIN murdered. Did you know that? I read it because I did my research. You should do your research. A lot of women don't know how to do research. They think that whatever some douche says on the news is real, but the truth is, there are a lot of different versions of the truth. Most women don't get that. Anyway, Hunter Biden is going to be arrested this week because of his laptop. You wait and see, it's happening. People are waking up. When they do, we can finally take back our country from the immigrants destroying us. Hey, how's that chicken? It's good here, right?" He says all this to me without pause.

The pinot noir goes down in one long, greedy, burning gulp. On our first date, he is wearing a zip-up sweatshirt and dirty jeans, as though he has just been working on a chain gang digging trenches. I am wearing dress pants and a lovely sweater with tasteful jewelry. My hair is blown out and looks great despite the drizzle, which can make me look like a cross between Barbra Streisand and Donna Summer in 1978. A well-worn ball cap on his head bears the logo of a local brewery, which he has mentioned he owns about forty times during the meal. The restaurant is a popular one on the south shore of Long Island. It is an Italian

My Year of Really Bad Dates

place with good sauce geared toward families. It is well-lit but not crowded on this rainy night. Do I retreat to the bathroom to deploy Plan B, the standby friend who can call to alert me to an emergency I must attend to immediately?

I was never good at figures, but I do some quick calculations in my head. Dating math, as I refer to it, requires a nimble mind and a working knowledge of physics, word problems, algebra and the ability to navigate between feet, inches, and meters. Tonight's equation is a tough one. If I am two-thirds done with my chicken Parm, and he is four-fifths through his pasta Madeira, and his height online was listed as six feet, how many more minutes do I have to wait until I can escape his actual five-foot-eight-inch frame as well as his barely double-digit IQ?

Not long, as it turns out. He is disenchanted with what he describes as my "woke" personality. If by "woke" he means I'm not sleeping, he's right about that. Score one for the dolt in the cap who has an irrational fear that drag queens will invade his brewery. I don't have the heart to tell him no self-respecting queen would come within a mile of the hole that is his pride and joy. In his profile, he listed his political views as moderate, though the conspiracy theories he has been throwing at me since he noticed the TV over the bar was tuned to CNN betray that his bend is slightly to the right of Attila the Hun. He whistles at the waitress and the poor woman being signaled to like a dog turns her head toward our table. He makes the universal sign for bringing the check by signing the air in front of him in a sweeping dramatic gesture. I'm almost out, and I exhale in relief. We exit together, and I thank him for dinner. He tries to kiss me on the lips, but I turn and offer him my cheek. He gets the message and stalks away without a goodbye.

Fair enough.

I'll never get those two hours back either, but there's no

Prologue

reason to be rude. It starts raining harder as I drive away and the drops bead on my windshield. For some reason, the rain has always made me amorous. My mind flashes to Joe, the man I had hoped to have a future with almost five years after I separated from my husband of twenty-two years, and our marathon lovemaking sessions in my bed while we listened to the rain on the roof and windows. After a year of dating, he joined a multilevel marketing self-help group and ended the relationship.

I shake the thought out of my head and hustle to make it home before eight thirty. My ex-husband will be dropping the kids off at my house any minute. In the eyes of the law, we are still married since he has employed every tactic to sign it out of existence. After he insisted on mediation and picked the mediator, which was fine by me, it has taken eighteen months to come to an agreement in which I receive nothing, waive child support, pay for college for both kids alone, and pay him alimony for five years. I can't fight him anymore on these issues, because he truly believes that he is under no obligation to pay for anything since he "can't." Of course, he "could," but that would require him to do things that he doesn't want to do, which never goes well for him. He has never been good with money and is the sort of man who my grandfather would have said "jumps over a dollar to pick up a dime." While this sounds better in Yiddish, I have never been able to convince him that his Ivy League education and the master's degree that I paid for could translate into earning a living.

While I was recovering from major abdominal surgery, I was blindsided by a letter from his "attorney of record," who underlined in red every aspect of the agreement where money was concerned, demanding more. The last paragraph of the document read something like: "If Rachel dies before his alimony is fully paid out, he has the right to take the remainder from her estate." Meaning, "If my ex-wife who supported me financially

My Year of Really Bad Dates

for twenty-two years drops dead from the stress and burden of responsibility that I have put on her for decades, I will steal the money I didn't earn from my children." When I read that, I collapsed onto the floor in a heap where I was found by a friend dropping off soup for my recovery. She picked me up off the floor, read the letter, and took me to her attorney's office that very afternoon.

That took another year, but we've about sorted that out finally. All we need to do now is file the final paper, but he won't respond to any letters, so eventually, I will have to hire a process server to physically serve him with the final documents. It's interesting to note that we live about eight blocks from one another, but I will still need to shell out more dough because every decision he makes in his life has a deleterious effect on me financially, emotionally, and in every other way a person can imagine.

We are in the middle of a text argument, the only way we communicate our anger these days. It's getting ugly and I want to be safely ensconced in my bedroom before he walks into my house like he lives there and we see one another face-to-face. It's my own home, which I purchased by myself, after our divorce with my own money. Yet, when I get home, I will cower in my bedroom upstairs to avoid a confrontation. I feel pathetic. Everything wrong in my life must be my fault because I am a terrible person, or so I now believe after decades of emotional and financial abuse and having to diminish myself to make everyone around me feel better about themselves. I used to live for confrontation. My father would always tell people I would surely be a lawyer because I loved arguing about anything and everything. But now, all the fight has been drained out of me. I am an empty shell of the person I once was, but I don't remember her now. It's just a hazy series of images, like watching clips on YouTube from some old television show I used to love but haven't thought about in years.

Prologue

My father is dead now. Seeing me like this would have killed him, or at least made him angry. I can hear his voice in my head: *What the hell is wrong with you? If you're going to act like a whiny baby, then you deserve to end up on the floor of your bedroom. Hey, are there any Twizzlers in here? I'm looking for a nosh.*

In a few months, I'll be fifty. I'm starting a new career as a writer while having full custody of my two teenagers with no break except Tuesday after school and Saturday between the hours of noon and six, though that is hazy too. Often, the kids will randomly show up when I'm supposed to be free. Once they showed up minutes after Joe and I had finished having great sex in the middle of the afternoon because my ex-husband had to "do something." Attempting to have some balance in my social life while juggling the rest has not been a resounding success. Since my ex-husband still lives in the large studio apartment that I procured for him when we separated, furnished mostly with the things I gave him, there is no room for the kids to hang out there for any length of time, let alone overnight. When I travel for work, he stays at my house. That's getting old too. Every time I come home from a trip, something in my house is broken, the kids are beating each other with household items, and general chaos has ensued in my absence.

Another really bad date has come and gone. As I pull into my driveway for the hundredth time, I vow to delete the dating apps for good and get a cat.

God, I fucking hate cats.

First Date

I NERVOUSLY AWAITED HIS ARRIVAL at the local bar in my neighborhood. This was my first time out since the breakup with Joe, the first man I dated seriously since my marriage ended. He left me to move out of state, and into a blond real estate agent with the IQ of an overripe turnip. He faulted me for not committing to him sooner and said that I was detached from my feelings. The idea of committing to another man I would have to care for terrified me, and now, I moved slowly in love and relationships. After nine months of dating exclusively, I decided that we could make a go of it for real. Before he left for a weeklong seminar in early September, I left a love note in his shaving kit, telling him I was excited about our future and couldn't wait for him to come home so we could talk. I had a whole evening planned that included my declaration of love, a suggestion that we start talking about living together, and great quickie sex in my closet before he had to get back to his condo to do his laundry and catch up at work for the week he missed.

My plan was quickly dashed when he came to my house directly from the airport, ate the dinner I made for him, and then told me he met a blond at the seminar, was moving to Phoenix, and was going to pursue a relationship with her instead.

You're not going to like this conversation.

He said this to me as I ushered him up the stairs to cover

First Date

him in kisses and tell him I loved him. Once again, the other shoe in my life had dropped. It has been raining shoes for the last forty-nine years. I'm drowning in dropped shoes. I should open a shoe store. I should open a chain of shoe stores. We had a conversation, but I don't remember much of it after his initial line.

As the saying goes, you don't always know what you have until it's gone. This time, however, I knew exactly what I had and wanted to keep it. Joe was not Mr. Saturday Night. He's not the flashy or showy or loud or attention-seeking type. He was the first man I ever dated to make me feel completely safe at any moment, and appreciated for exactly who and what I am. Also, for what I am not. I'm not even sure he understood what moved me about him, which was his gentle but simultaneously very strong masculinity, warmth, curiosity, and understated humor. He's quiet until you know him, but once you get him talking, he is up to discuss anything and everything. Being with him was always easy. Whether we were going away for a weekend or on a trip to the hardware store, we always had a good time. I found even his strangest of quirks interesting and adorable, like how he has his special mitt to handwash his car because, as he explained to me, the sand and dirt on the carwash brushes are gross. He was never persnickety, precious, or preachy about these aspects of his personality, but rather, he had done the research, experimented, learned, and now uses his own.

As for being detached, hell yes, I have always been detached from my feelings. We don't run much to actual core feelings in my family. Rather, we prefer the New York Jewish method of communication, which is to scream our opinions to the person who happens to be sitting closest. Whoever yells the loudest gets their feelings semi-validated or, at least, acknowledged first. I own that. There hasn't been space to feel much of anything in the last few years. Between the end of my twenty-two-year marriage, my father's sudden death, and his girlfriend suing me within an inch of my life, not to mention sole custody of my kids, feelings have been relegated to the back burner. I've been trying now since Joe left. I realized that I wanted to tell him I loved him months earlier, but I was afraid that he didn't feel the same, that I'd be hurt, that saying "I love you" would mean a host of other things I couldn't even begin to sort out in my addled mind.

SUDDENLY, BEING ON A DATE felt too soon. I was still hurting, and I needed more time. But since my girlfriend, a therapist, accused me of being love avoidant, I went on the date to prove otherwise. Besides, I'm not convinced love avoidant is a thing. If it is a thing, I don't think I qualify. I prefer to think of myself as love adjacent. But really, I went to show Joe that I didn't care. *I'll find another, better Joe. Joe 2.0, in a heartbeat. I'll show him,* I thought. He met a woman that he committed to in five days (which I thought and still think is insane). I could fall in love with a random stranger too! I ordered a pinot noir to warm me up and calm me down before my date arrived. There was a chill in the October air. Fall had arrived in New York.

Waiting for him to arrive, I cycled through the myriad of first dates that I'd had in my life. I was never a great dater. Most of the long-term relationships I'd had were born out of friendship. I was what used to be called a late bloomer. In high school, I was the girl that boys wanted to joke around with, not take to dances or make out with in their cars. My great teenage romances were with gay men. I like baseball and basketball, though my lifelong support of both the Mets and the Knicks has mostly led to heartbreak. I'm not a jealous person, and I'm not sure if I truly believe that monogamy is the only way to go through life. I love bourbon, dark humor, and lots of other things that have traditionally

First Date

been considered in the masculine domain. This has always led to strong and deep connections and friendships with men. My college boyfriends all started as pals. My first date with my husband was in 1996, and I had known him for years. I didn't even know it was a date since he originally asked me to do him a favor and attend a staged reading of a play at some hotel in Los Angeles that his father had starred in on Broadway in the eighties. He had not brought a girl around in some time, and his family was starting to wonder if he was some kind of homosexual (not that there's anything wrong with that) hermit. We closed the bar that night and stayed together for twenty-five years. Our bond was our love of dark humor and the trauma we had both endured as children with chilly, distant mothers and fathers who abandoned us for greener pastures. They couldn't stand the women they had married but had no problems leaving us to deal with them alone. My last first date was with Joe in January of 2022, and we made out in the vestibule of the restaurant until management kicked us out to lock up.

I had no illusions that this first date would be a winner. I'm not even sure I wanted it to be, but I didn't have time to spin further out of control in my mind because he arrived just as I was about to hyperventilate. I recognized him from his pictures online, which was a great sign. Though he was a bit shorter than he described, an inch or two off is considered acceptable when it comes to dating math. He smiled and sat down, ordered a beer, and we started chatting. He had a pleasant voice: not too high, and not too husky and low. He was the baby bear of the dating voice and just right—another good sign. Sometimes men, especially white men, put on a Barry White sexy voice when they initially engage. I'm told that the female inverse is vocal fry. Physically speaking, vocal fry is the shortening of vocal folds, so they close completely and then snap back open. The result is a frying or sizzling sound. From a

My Year of Really Bad Dates

cultural perspective, this phenomenon has best been described as how a Kardashian speaks. In addition to all the other issues one must take into consideration when dating in the twenty-first century, speech-pattern analysis is now included.

I asked what should have been an innocuous question:

"How often do you date?"

"Well, I haven't been on a date in a while," he replied.

"What's 'a while'?"

"Well, my wife and I met in middle school."

I knew I was in trouble five and a half minutes into the date.

He proceeded to drop another bomb by telling me that he and his wife were still living together. "See, I live in the basement now, and she's in our bedroom. She has a new boyfriend now. Well, he's not new. I mean, I know the guy. He was my business partner and best friend for the last thirty years." His smile was casual, almost nonchalant, as he shared his story.

I'm not sure where he expected the date to go after revealing his situation. I could tell he was sweet, and I felt terrible for him, but I also glanced at my phone and realized that soon, the nightly reruns of classic sitcoms would air on METV. I think on Tuesdays they show *Taxi*, one of my all-time favorites. This is the one night of the week I don't have to make dinner or check homework. My ex-husband picks the kids up from school and takes my son to his dance class, and my daughter goes to whichever play she is in rehearsal for on Tuesdays. Of course, I ended up with a theater kid and a competitive dancer. They get their remarkable skills and talent from him and his side of the family. I'd like to believe they got their brains and ability to speak fluent sarcasm from me. All these thoughts swirled in my head while I continued to listen to his sob story.

My instinct was to help him, but I wasn't sure if I wanted to help him because I liked him and had empathy or because

First Date

I'd spent my entire life diminishing my own needs to take care of another man's feelings. I spent my childhood constantly worried about my father. He lived on the edge of the law, fixing horse races, running card games, lending money, and engaging in other nefarious small-time illegal activities alone in a series of dumpy apartments that he would switch out every eighteen months or so to avoid being detected by the various people and groups who might have been following him. He dated a series of awful women, each worse than the last, and even married a few. He often would tell me that I was the only person in the world he could ever fully trust, and I took that burden very seriously throughout his lifespan. I think I was seven the first time he uttered that sentence. Maybe six. My greatest childhood fear was that he would be killed and I would be left alone in the world. I lived with my mother. She clothed me and fed me and made sure I ate something green a few times a week, but she didn't trust me to use her hairbrush. Having a conversation with her was next to impossible, especially since she was typically too exhausted to hear anything I had to say. My father, the two days a week I spent with him, was present. He didn't mind me asking him ten thousand questions about everything and nothing. He never spoke to me like I was a kid, but rather as a peer or pal. Despite his many faults, as a child, I believed that he was the only person whom I could ever fully love and trust.

My ex-husband had a nervous breakdown two months after we walked down the aisle after a year of his parents ignoring his impending nuptials and behaving abominably at his wedding. He later confessed that our marriage allowed him to feel safe enough to let himself deal with his traumatic childhood: abandoned by his famous father, disabused of the notion that he mattered and was a part of his dad's life by his unkind stepmother who saw his existence as a threat, and emotionally abused by his mentally ill, addicted mom from birth. When he recovered enough to hold a lengthy conversation, he told me that he finally let himself fall apart once we were legally married because he knew that I'd take care of him and never leave. The irony of being his safety while he never once acted as mine has only recently dawned on me. He spent two years crying and attending Al-Anon and deep therapy while I worked four jobs to keep us afloat. After our wedding, he never earned a steady paycheck to contribute to our household regularly. That became my job alone. I taught UCLA night school, I was the CEO of the Los Angeles Museum of the Holocaust (now Holocaust Museum LA), I worked as an oral historian interviewing children suffering from chronic pain for an NIH grant I helped write, and on weekends I worked at Barnes & Noble. That went on until two weeks before I gave birth to my first child, which was four years into the marriage. I was nine months and one week pregnant when I quit two of my side jobs and kept my full-time gig as the CEO of the Los Angeles Museum of the Holocaust.

After intensive help and intervention, he pulled out of it and earned a master's degree that I paid for, but depression is an odious foe. Its cyclical pattern continued to haunt us, plunging our lives into financial instability, insecurity, and emotional chaos for the remainder of our twenty-two years together. Our families, unequipped and equally uninterested in understanding the situation, got angrier with what they perceived as each failure on our part when the disease reared its ugly head; often, we ended up making decisions in panic mode, which does not lead to great life choices. Essentially, each family threw up their hands and left us twisting in the wind. I had no training on or understanding about how to deal with the situation, so I approached it as though I was learning on the job. The problem was that I had never received a job description when I applied. What was

First Date

the job? Caretaker? Mother? Wife? Unwanted daughter-in-law? Partner? Bringer of the Kosher bacon? I was suddenly all those things without a manual or training session. All newlyweds have an adjustment period, but we had no honeymoon phase. We went from walking down the aisle in joy to immobile on the sofa without a clue within two months. It became my job to manage what felt unmanageable.

MY THOUGHTS TURNED BACK to my date for the evening. This man needed help, and since I was the one sitting next to him that evening, I decided to try. I took a deep breath.

"I'm sorry this is happening, but if you want my honest opinion, I don't think you're quite ready to hit the dating scene or be on the train wreck that is the average dating app."

He seemed unnerved and said, "You think? But she has someone. I should too."

"Sure, but maybe some therapy? It can be very helpful. Or at least get a place of your own. It might be awkward to bring a woman to the basement of the home you're paying for and hiding out in from your ex-wife and business partner."

"And best friend!" he added, still grinning. "Don't forget that part!"

"Oh, I haven't forgotten that part. But honestly, I feel like it might be a bit too soon for you. I went through a breakup myself pretty recently, and I think it may be too soon for me."

He looked disappointed that the date would not end the way he hoped. He was cute and engaging, and if his life wasn't a complete disaster, he would have gotten a second date. Rather than improve his mood, my words of encouragement seemed to plunge him into further despair. I suddenly worried that he would cry, right there in the bar.

My Year of Really Bad Dates

I have never dealt well with crying. My parents hated it when I cried and would scream at me to stop or accuse me of being dramatic and crying for attention. My in-laws would scream and yell at me on a fairly regular basis and seemed to get a kick out of humiliating me in public and private. When my husband's stepmother would scream in my face and call me truly vile names ("You and your husband are fucking asshole pieces of shit!") I would start to cry, which infuriated her further. After the first few years of these horrific confrontations, I was able to control the crying and would simply silently weep in the bar, in the lobby of the hotel, in the street, in their kitchen, or over the phone. After many years, I managed to stop crying altogether, swallowing the enormous lump in my throat that was so big it hurt and burned badly when I squeezed it down. It has gotten to the point where I cannot express emotions around most people because I have been trained to swallow them all, especially the crying.

It took me years to understand that my ex-husband never took a stand for me because he could never take a stand for himself when he was being yelled at or gaslit either. How could he protect me when nobody ever protected him? When I took my first CEO job in New York, I had a handwritten sign on my office door that read simply: *You May Not Cry in Here.* By the time my husband moved out, I was so ill from swallowing emotions that I had two enormous hernias which had become vascular, tangling my intestines, and a bleeding ulcer that required surgery. To this day, I don't even do well when my kids cry for an extended period; by *extended*, I mean more than three minutes.

Thankfully, he didn't cry. We finished our drinks, and he graciously paid the check, though I offered to go Dutch. He walked me to my car, parked only a few feet from the bar's front door. It was an awkward moment. I knew I would never see him again. He was fragile and lonely, but I was looking for a partner or at

First Date

least a boyfriend, not a project. I smiled at him as I went to open the door, and he swept me into his arms and kissed me, ramming his tongue into my mouth and down my throat hard and fast. He saw me as the first new woman he had kissed since 1987 and figured it was now or never. Either that, or he was practicing for a CPR class at the local YMCA. Regardless, he was a terrible kisser, all tongue and saliva, no tenderness, passion, or regard for the mouth he entered. The tongue bandit's roughness brought my goodwill to its inevitable end. I groped behind my back for the car's door handle, got inside, and pulled away as quickly as I could without running him down. I saw him smile and wave confidently in my rearview mirror as I screeched toward home around the block.

    I congratulated myself for driving instead of walking, while simultaneously cursing myself for going out. Not only did I miss *Taxi*, but I had my tonsils examined by a stranger. I don't even like it when my primary care doctor, whom I adore, asks me to say "ah" and lays the wooden stick on my tongue. I do love kissing. It's one of my favorite things when I'm doing it with someone that I'm into. I've been lucky to have experienced some great kissers. The childhood crush that I had a torrid affair with during my open-marriage days was world-class. It was my ex-husband's idea, and I wanted to please him, and maybe get one or two of my own needs met for a change. Steve, my long-term boyfriend from that period with whom I spent fantastic, sweat-filled nights in hotel rooms all over Manhattan every six to eight weeks for almost a decade, was another award winner. Joe and I would make out constantly, and it was an incredible turn-on. My ex-husband wasn't bad in that department either, but I cannot remember what it was like to be intimate with him. I know for a fact that all these men loved me, and still love me as best they can, but they were doomed from the start despite the incredible chemistry and passion that I had with each of them since there was no way they could ever commit to me. It turns out I am not the "love 'em and leave 'em" type, as much as I wanted to be hip and cool and make my marriage work.

I always seem to pick the wrong man. When Joe left, I finally realized that something inside me must be broken. Historically, I had a clear type. He was hilarious, handsome, tall, dark, brooding, insanely talented, charismatic, emotionally ruined, withholding, and incapable of any kind of commitment or ability to choose me for the long haul. I thought I had chosen differently when I started to date Joe, but he withheld from me just like the rest in the end. I had no idea he believed I was emotionally detached. He never once brought it up.

AS I PULLED INTO THE DRIVEWAY after this first date, I was looking forward to a hot bath and the third of a joint I had been saving for a special occasion. I made my way up my front stairs and entered the house only to find my two teenage children facing each other in a gladiator stance. My fourteen-year-old son had a spatula and was wielding it like a sword. My seventeen-year-old daughter was attempting to fight him off with a couch cushion. My son is a competitive dancer, lithe as a grasshopper. My daughter is a theater kid on the spectrum known for falling to the floor when sitting at the table eating dinner. Her coordination has never been stellar, and she often trips over herself. She was no match for his moves. At first, I wasn't sure if they were joking around, but the screaming indicated that it was a deadly serious skirmish. I couldn't tell who ate the last ice cream sandwich or which one of them used the other's shampoo, but either way, I arrived home just in time to avoid bloodshed. I snatched the spatula out of his hand just before he brought it down on her wrist. With the other

First Date

hand, I grabbed her cushion, lost my balance, and fell on the tile floor flat on my back. In addition to my wilting self-esteem, it felt as though I'd fractured my spine as I lay on the floor wondering how I had ended up here at this point in my life.

Once I untangled the argument and got them to agree not to murder one another—and cleaned up the mess they left behind—it felt too late to run a bath and luxuriate. The children were banished to their rooms, and I heard them grumbling about fairness and favoritism as I went through my nighttime ablutions. I smoked the jay on my tiny terrace, and it was just what I needed. It had been a long evening and I needed to unwind. I crawled into bed just in time for *Cheers*. It was the episode where Coach, about to attend his best friend's memorial service at the bar, finds out he hit on his wife, and he feels blindsided and devastated. I empathized with him. Just as I was drifting off, I got a text message from Joe:

Falling asleep. Thinking of you.

I decided to hold off on dating until I felt a little more grounded and a little less messy.

The One with Potential

OCTOBER TURNED TO NOVEMBER, which meant my least favorite holiday was upon me. I have always hated Thanksgiving. It is a lot of work for a meal that typically lasts about twenty minutes before whichever family you are with breaks out into total dysfunction. When we were married, my husband and I always went away for Thanksgiving. It was too painful not to be included at our fathers' holiday tables. My father's girlfriend only allowed her own family to come for Thanksgiving, citing her lack of chairs as the excuse. On the surface, she was a sweet, genteel lady who cared for my father. But her behavior over the years belied her real interest, which was control. She didn't like the way he dressed or the car he drove, which did not reflect the image that she and her shallow family liked to portray. She didn't like his friends and wouldn't allow them to socialize in the home they shared in Buffalo, New York. He would have to go to them or go out somewhere public to meet them. She did not want to live in a penthouse condo but wanted a stand-alone home in a gated golfing community. My father hated golf but relented and paid for the prefab ugly home and the astonishing cost of a golf club membership for the privilege of eating in the dining room twice a week and being served by the waitstaff—the only people of color, seemingly, allowed on the hallowed

The One with Potential

property. Holidays were her domain for her family only, where she would decorate with enormous garish nutcrackers, life-sized Easter bunnies, and other atrocious seasonal décor. He would bitterly complain about the *chazeri* (Yiddish for useless bric-a-brac) but continued to shell out the dollars to pay for all of it regardless of his kvetching.

My ex-husband's father simply never invited us once we left Los Angeles in 2007. The few times we inquired about their plans, we were told they were spending a quiet holiday, just his father and stepmother, at a restaurant, only to discover on Facebook that his siblings and their partners were devouring turkeys and racks of lamb the size of tables with them at their beautiful vacation home. After the inevitable Facetime call, my kids would ask why everyone in Daddy's family was together except Daddy. I spent years telling them it was because I had to work, and they would cry and tell me I was a mean mommy. It was never discussed, and no apologies or explanations were ever offered. I dared to bring it up once, when his brother, eleven years his junior, called me to verbally assault me over the phone for some reason that was never made clear to me. I dared to ask him what the heck was going on and why we were never included.

"Who do you think you are?" the then twenty-four-year-old, who to this day has never once inquired about his niece or nephew, replied. "There isn't enough room for you. There aren't enough beds."

I explained to him that I had in fact been to their vacation house and that there were in fact plenty of beds. He hung up on me. After calling me a cunt. We spent several Thanksgiving weekends in Pennsylvania at Hersheypark eating at the buffet and riding roller coasters in the cold. Those times were memorable but always a little sad for the family we could not have.

My Year of Really Bad Dates

GIVEN THE DEPRESSING TIME OF YEAR, it was not surprising that my earlier decision to hold off on dating did not last. My decision not to date never lasted. I like men. I like their company; I like lying next to a man I love and talking to him lazily as I drift off. I like hearing about his day. And I like sex. The idea of not having a regular sex life after having a great one for the last year upset me. I had an idea that if I could fix the external, the internal would fall into place.

Less than a week later, I received a message from Mark on the app, which I had only checked once that week. He was six foot five, published a magazine, and might have been the best-looking man I had ever seen on a dating app. His message was irreverent, warm, and confident without being cocky. This is a rarity in the dating-app world, like a digital needle in a phony haystack built on a throne of lies. We traded app messages for several days before I decided he wasn't a serial killer and he decided I wasn't insane. We gave one another our phone numbers and exchanged text messages for another few days. Two weeks into our virtual conversation, we decided to take the first big leap and spoke on the phone. The conversation lasted for an hour. He was smart and funny with a sexy voice, and I learned that in addition to writing, he was also a painter. He was handy and did most of the work on his small house by himself. As a bonus, he lived in the Finger Lakes region. For that moment in time, dating someone who lived four hours away seemed to me the perfect arrangement in my clear mess of a mind. I could get the feelings, have some fun, and take things at my glacial pace without committing simply because of the distance. It seemed the ideal situation. The last online-dating hurdle loomed large: Should we meet in person? He had a publisher's conference about two hours away from

The One with Potential

me and suggested we get together. If we clicked, I'd be delighted. I was convinced I needed to move on and put myself back out there. The worst-case scenario wasn't so bad either. If he turned out to be a dud in person, I could still spend a night in a hotel room alone, which was an unknown dimension to me. It felt like a win-win, so I agreed, and we set the meeting for the week after Thanksgiving.

I fielded text messages from all the exes in my life that holiday week: ex-husband, ex-boyfriend, and even an old friend I had not heard from in over a year. Cute-screenwriter Paul, a part of my online Clubhouse writers' group that I had a little crush on, sent me funny memes of turkeys, and we both agreed that the "Turkey Drop" episode of *WKRP in Cincinnati* was the greatest twenty-two minutes of television ever written. We watched it virtually together while I made mashed potatoes to bring to the feast. My college roommate and best friend Lynn lived around the corner with her family, and the kids and I spent Thanksgiving there. I showed her Mark's picture and she approved.

We spoke every day leading up to the meeting and talked about our craving for intimacy and our heartbreak over the ends of our marriages.

AS I PREPARED TO MEET MARK, Joe texted from Phoenix, where he had spent Thanksgiving, asking me to meet him at the diner where we had our first meeting to decide if we liked each other enough to go on a proper date. He said he missed me and wanted to see me, which made my heart skip a beat. Maybe he realized what a mistake he was making by leaving me. I dressed in his favorite outfit and wore my new stiletto thigh-high boots that I had bought right before he left me as a surprise, since I knew he had a thing for me in high heels. I felt a little foolish in

My Year of Really Bad Dates

a mini-skirt and thigh-high boots in a Long Island diner on a dreary, rainy night, but I was trying to convey a message to him that said, *I am everything you want! Pick me!* But instead of telling me he wanted me back, he revealed that he'd purchased a home in Phoenix and showed me photos.

"You bought this house. Why did you call me? Why did you want to see me?" I asked him, genuinely confused.

"Because I wanted to see you. I missed you," was his reply.

I felt like an idiot. I ended up crying on his shoulder in the parking lot. He held me tight and told me he still wasn't sure he was making the right decision and that he may yet change his mind. I was totally confused and heartbroken. I drove home in tears and told myself that Mark was going to be great and that I should stop crying. I choked back the tears as I had been trained to do. The lump was getting so hard to swallow that I gagged and had to pull over in case I vomited. I was pretty sure this was our last goodbye, and I was miserable, but I told myself it was done and vowed not to text him.

Days later, I headed down the elevator from my hotel room and found Mark waiting in the lobby. He was handsome and his smile was so engaging it seemed like being in a bad mood around this man would be impossible. We walked to the restaurant, and he took my hand in his, which startled me. Nobody had held my hand for months, and at that moment, I realized how much I missed the feeling. While we ate, we chatted over this and that. During our month of communication before our meeting, we talked about sex and love and all kinds of things, including whether we would spend the night together. All the signs over the meal pointed to yes, though each one of us was too self-conscious and shy to bring up the topic first. We lingered over the meal, and I even went so far as to order coffee after dinner, which I never do. After three hours, it became clear that

The One with Potential

it was time to leave and he walked me back to my hotel, kissing me on the street.

Surprisingly, the kiss was not great. It was tight, thin-lipped, and dry. It seemed perfunctory. I was disappointed, but I thought he might have been nervous and would calm down and ease into a better one next time, so I invited him upstairs. It had been months since I'd had sex and there was a part of me that felt like I needed to go ahead and get over the hump, so to speak, but I was a nervous wreck. We sat on the bed and talked for a while, and though I was attracted to him, something held me back. He had brought up his overnight bag from his car, and as we talked, he told me that he needed to get ready for our encounter. What was he getting ready for? In my experience, getting ready equaled taking off your clothes, but that was not the case for him. From his overnight case, he produced a huge Ziplock bag filled with colorful round objects from the full rainbow.

"I told you I've had some issues since my divorce in this department, right?" he asked.

He had, but he'd left out a few wee details.

"Wearing a cock ring is the best way for me to stay hard. Also, I can only cum if you sit on my face and stroke my cock. Don't worry, I'll show you." The hotel had provided a fruit bowl and he grabbed a banana, ostensibly to show me what he meant.

I was worried. I froze up.

He must have sensed that something was wrong because he immediately suggested that we take the pressure off and just lie down together and talk and cuddle. I was instantly relieved and so that is exactly how we spent the next eight hours. He fell asleep, but I lay awake most of the night.

What the hell am I doing here? I asked myself. *I don't want to be here. I want to be in my bed at home with Joe watching* Mystery Science Theater 3000 *while the dog snores between us.* I knew that I was being cold and distant, and I couldn't figure out why. I was attracted to him, but I found his sexual rules and regulations off-putting, rigid, and not particularly romantic. Also, it was a lot about him and his penis. While I understood that the penis was an intrinsic part of the coupling itself, it was also supposed to be about the journey and the process. I'd also hoped it might be a bit of fun, but the singular focus on his penis sucked the joy right out of the whole thing.

WE WOKE UP IN THE morning and fooled around. I was hopeful in the cold gray light of early morning that he would relax and forget about his little bag of tricks, but he did not and went right to it, rummaging through to find a particularly offensive orange ring. It wasn't big, but it was the color of a pumpkin, and without being too graphic, it looked very well-worn. The idea of my lady bits rubbing up on God knows how many other lady bits, even with the condom, gave me the creeps. We managed the act itself. I did not enjoy it. Though I wanted to, it felt like I was following a series of step-by-step instructions to put together a piece of Ikea furniture as he talked me through exactly what he needed.

"Harder. No, slower. Gentler. Linger on the head for a minute. Like this; up and down!" He put his hand over mine and moved it up and down. I felt like Daniel-san in the creepy version of *The Karate Kid*.

We took a quick, awkward shower and decided to get a cup of coffee together before we parted ways. He told me he was super into me. Once the sexual tension had dissipated, in a disappointing way for me, I found myself enjoying his company. He was relaxed, easygoing, smart, and interesting. We had a lot in common, and I liked him a lot more by the time we left. I wondered if he was worth further investment. Perhaps he was nervous? Maybe

The One with Potential

after getting to know one another, things would be easier. I had a lot to think about as I drove home in the rain. I wondered why it was always raining when I went on first dates. Was it a sign?

I listened to the Sinatra station, and "One for My Baby (and One More for the Road)" started. Its melancholy and simple piano opening has always moved me, and it's one of my favorite songs. In it, Sinatra pours his heart out to Joe the bartender over the last call, telling him how his relationship ended while trying to sound casual, as though he doesn't care. He cares. It is the magic of the song and of Sinatra himself. I started to cry, which was odd because, as you may remember, I am not a crier. Especially not over songs, movies, or television commercials. Though he hated it when I cried, my father used to bawl at movies. Once when we went to see the (terrible) remake of *Little Women* with Wynona Ryder, a movie he went to kicking and screaming, I thought he had fallen asleep when suddenly I heard a wail beside me.

"Oh God, Beth. No. You can't die! Not Beth!"

His then-wife and I looked at one another and moved down the row.

This time, however, when I went to swallow the lump, I couldn't. It was too big to swallow. And the tears came. Great big ones that uncomfortably soaked my face, and though I willed them to stop as I had always been trained to do, this time, I couldn't control them, and they flowed for what seemed an eternity. When I pulled over to gas up the car, I broke my vow and texted the song to Joe, the ex-boyfriend, not the bartender, and told him I was thinking of him. He responded immediately and told me he thought about me all the time too. He told me he was confused. He told me he loved me. I reopened the cycle and I hated doing it, but I couldn't help myself. Somewhere in my disturbed mind, I just knew that if he chose me, if he decided that I was the love of his life and the one he wanted to be with, everything would be right in the world. His

My Year of Really Bad Dates

choosing me would make up for every man that had never chosen me as their priority or person, from my father to my ex-husband to the various men I had spent twenty-five years working for, all the while diminishing myself to make each man and male-dominated board feel more secure. They were always the ones in charge, and I was just the window dresser who did the leg work and took the hits on their behalf.

By the time I got home, I had a rare moment of clarity, and I texted Mark:

Hey Mark. I just wanted to let you know I was home.

Hey you! I can't wait to see you again, he texted right back.

You are a terrific man, but I don't think we are a good match. I'm happy to call and discuss it further, but I don't see this working long-term.

Thirty minutes went by, and I wasn't sure I would hear from him again. Just as I was making dinner, I received his response:

Not necessary to hop on a call. I think you're right. You're a cold fish, and while you are gorgeous and smart and sexy, you don't get my situation, and you're a lousy lay.

This response took me aback. I am not good at a lot of things, but sex isn't one of them. I have always received compliments in this arena from the men in my life. It isn't as though there have been legions or myriads, but there have been enough to validate that I know what I'm doing in that department. When not faced with used cock rings, I am downright adventurous and fun to go to bed with, and I am comfortable in my skin and body. For me, sex is as much a mental game as a physical one, and I feel agile there as well. I could easily have thrown a barb about his sexual issues, but I stopped myself. There was no reason to engage in a battle of wits. He was a decent, handsome, nice man, but he wasn't for me, and that was the end of that. I deleted his number and reminded myself that the first time out of the gate, sleeping

The One with Potential

with someone new was bound to be strange. I reasoned that now that I had that first one under my belt, dating and pursuing a sex life would become much easier. The next time I met someone great that I was attracted to, it would be smooth sailing. I wasn't sure I was fully on board with this thought process, but I was trying to convince myself that next time, it would be terrific. But would it? My grandmother always said there was a lid for every pot (again, it sounds better in Yiddish), but maybe I was the pot without a lid. Maybe broken pots never find the lids that fit.

The Next Marc

IT WAS A FEW WEEKS before Christmas, just after the cockring episode, and I got right back on the apps in the hopes that I could have a merry Christmas or at least a decent date. When Marc walked into the coffee shop, I couldn't believe my luck. He was much better looking in person than he was in his photos. And he was fine as hell in those. He was tall, with dark wavy hair with strands of salt and pepper shot through. He was broad and confident and had a very dry sense of humor. We had a terrific coffee and I kicked myself that our time together was so rushed. Since we were both a little burned out from online dating, we had agreed to grab a quick coffee to see if there was enough to warrant a full-on date. I wished we could have spent more time together because I wouldn't be able to see him again until I got back from Europe. It was Sean's fiftieth birthday, my ride or die since the age of fourteen, and his closest friends were meeting in Paris and then heading to Corsica to celebrate the occasion. The week was arranged by his husband, whom I also adore. I had been looking forward to this trip since the summer, though there was a part of me that was also sad. Joe was supposed to go with me on this trip.

We left the coffee shop, and I walked Marc through the Union Square Christmas Market, where he was looking for gifts

The Next Marc

to bring to Germany. He went each year to visit his folks who still lived there, though he had lived in the United States for almost thirty years. As we walked, he spotted mistletoe hanging from a lamppost. He smiled broadly, swept me up in his big strong arms, and kissed me passionately in the middle of the market as a light snow began to fall. It was a fantastic kiss. I felt like the star of my own Hallmark movie. When I opened my eyes again, I was even standing in front of a cupcake-and-cocoa stand in the market, the center point of every piece of treacle Hallmark produces. It was intoxicating, and as we parted company, I felt lightheaded. We liked each other so much that we made plans for New Year's Eve. In the ensuing weeks, we built up to the excitement of seeing one another again, and I liked that we took our time to keep getting to know each other over the phone and text before our next in-person date. I was still talking to other men online, but I finally had a really great date under my belt, which slightly restored my faith in the process. Marc and I texted daily, getting flirtier and sexier. The night before I left for Paris, he texted:

I realize this may be inappropriate, but I have such a good feeling about you that I'll say it outright: I can't wait to fuck you and I plan to be the best you ever had. You are magnificent.

I giggled like a schoolgirl as I read his message. Nobody had ever described me as magnificent before. Nobody ever really complimented me much in my life. As vulgar as it was, the text message felt like an oxygen infusion.

THE WEEK IN EUROPE WAS a welcome respite. There is nothing like being in the company of your favorite people to anchor yourself when you feel unmoored, and though I couldn't even acknowledge it to myself at the time, in retrospect I was fully adrift at sea. I wasn't sleeping much and was constantly checking

My Year of Really Bad Dates

my phone to see if Joe had texted and was thinking about me. A man who left me unceremoniously five days after meeting another woman. I should have just deleted his number, but I couldn't. Joe had become my validation, and losing him so quickly was like getting the wind knocked out of me. It had taken me so long to get there with Joe, and I still couldn't quite believe it was over. I always felt, and still feel, that Joe and I did things the right way. We took our time, got to know one another, and established something meaningful, which was probably why his sudden departure was so painful. It wasn't just about the great sex, though we had a lot of that; there was a real foundation there as well. Or so I thought.

Marc was getting a bit more daring as well, sharing the things he wanted to do to me and with me. I missed sex and intimacy and fun and being a little dirty with someone who was into me. I met him where he was, though we stopped short of photo swapping or incredibly intimate information. He was game, but I like to discover things for myself, and he agreed.

In Paris and Corsica, I ate everything and drank even more. Between the morning mimosas, the afternoon chardonnay, and the Corsican whiskey that was broken out around four each afternoon (smoky, smooth, and extraordinary), I was perpetually slightly inebriated for five straight days. We danced, laughed, and explored the magnificent island of Corsica, all while staying at a brand-new hotel Sean's friends were about to open. We were the soft-launch guinea pigs, and boy, did they do a phenomenal job with the place. Corsican separatists had blown up the property fifteen years earlier, and after buying the rubble, they created a stunning space at Villa Flaka Cargese (I cannot wait to return, which I plan to do as soon as possible).

Late one night, Joe texted and bemoaned the fact that he wasn't with me. Marc also kept in touch. His aging parents were driving him bananas and he told me that thinking about me and

The Next Marc

what I would be like naked in his arms was a wonderful distraction. Sean and Kazim encouraged me to stop communicating with Joe and move on to find someone "worthy." They, along with Jim, who could not make the trip, have known me and my disastrous love life since I was a teenager. They love me and always want what is best for me, and though I knew this intellectually, I couldn't seem to stop my self-destructive behavior.

When I returned from Europe right before the New Year, I had a nasty cold that I couldn't shake. Marc came home in time for New Year's Eve under the weather as well, so instead of going out on the town as we'd planned, we decided to postpone our next encounter until we were both feeling better. Joe spent Christmas and New Year's in Phoenix and texted me daily the entire time he was gone. He implied that he would decide what to do when he returned home and that he missed me. He seemed distressed when I told him I had a date for New Year's Eve and encouraged me to "keep it light" until he got home and we could sit down and talk.

Are you going to sleep with him?

I have no idea. I think not. Are you going to sleep with your blond?

I'm going to sleep on my sister's couch and kiss my nephews!

He didn't even mention the blond. I broke down and told him I was sick and canceled the date, and he sent me that weird emoji where the yellow smiley has a bead of sweat falling down the side of its maniacal face. I spent a hopeful night in bed with my kids and we watched the Miley Cyrus and Dolly Parton special. I was thrilled it ended with "Jolene."

MARC AND I FINALLY MET UP the second week of the New Year when we were feeling better. We chose a romantic little out-of-the-way restaurant on the east side. It was beautiful and the

My Year of Really Bad Dates

food fabulous. He took my hand. We were clearly attracted to one another, and the vibe was great. By our second date, we had been talking and building up the moment for a month, and it felt like I knew him, which of course was ridiculous. I didn't know this man at all, but again, being adrift is typically not a great state in which to make judgments about anything.

We went back to my hotel room and spent the night together. The sex was just okay, which was a bummer because he'd talked himself up there. A lot. We woke up and grabbed breakfast and coffee in the hotel. It was a beautiful winter morning in New York City, and the sun was streaming through the windows in the breakfast room, which we had all to ourselves. Over coffee, I asked him what he was looking for moving forward in his life. He told me he was ultimately looking for a partner though what that looked like wasn't yet clear to him. I told him I was looking for the same, and that while I looked, I wanted to enjoy dating again. I told him I would be in the city again in two weeks if he wanted to grab a drink or coffee.

This was not a marriage proposal. Nor was it an idea to go steady. I didn't ask him to put his French Club pin on my sweater. It was coffee or a drink. I was not suggesting a lifetime of monogamy or even trying to set a time for our next date. The minute I mentioned coffee or a drink, his face went blank. I knew immediately that there was something wrong.

"I need to process our evening. Let me get back to you on that," he said.

Process? His language was supposed to be gentle and give off the impression that he had depth. He'd failed epically. I said goodbye and we parted company.

He texted over the next few days, making casual chitchat and small talk. On day three, he texted me the following:

Good evening. You are a smart, wonderful, attractive, and sexy woman but I am not feeling love for you. I cannot be what you are

The Next Marc

looking for, and I think we should not communicate further. You deserve a committed, dedicated man, but that man cannot be me at this time. I am confident that because of your tremendous assets, you will soon find the right man to marry who will treat you the way you deserve to be treated. I wish I was ready to be that man for you. Alas, don't worry, I have every confidence your mister right is around the corner!

I could tell that I was not the first woman who was texted that speech. I am also willing to bet money that he kept it in the notes section of his phone and had merely cut and pasted it into a text message. It was clear to me that his belief system was that all women over the age of thirty-five are dating to trap themselves a man. His arrogance and mansplaining of my needs turned my stomach and infuriated me. It took me a few minutes to collect myself, but I finally responded by telling him I was not looking for someone terrific to marry. I also told him that his chutzpah was astounding and that not one thing he had said about my needs and desires was accurate. As for the implication that over two months and two dates I was somehow in love with him, I described that as laughable. I ended the text with the line:

You should get some new material. Women are not one-size-fits-all. Besides, the sex wasn't good enough for a callback.

I saw the three dots flash as if he was responding, and then they disappeared. I saw them again, and then they disappeared. I saw this several more times before I finally realized there was no point in even reading what this man had to say, and I deleted his contact. Then I deleted the dating app on which we met.

I'm too old for this shit, I thought. Being alone was preferable to dealing with arrogant man-children who didn't know who they were, what they wanted, or where they were going. If one more man told me who I was, what I thought and felt, and what I needed, I was going to commit a felony. I needed to get off "the apps," but I always went back. It wasn't exactly obsessive, but I spent much more time than I should have swiping terrible profiles with my finger. It was becoming the thing I did at night before I went to sleep, and it was doing nothing to set my mind straight.

My dreams were getting darker, and I knew what was coming. I had haunting dreams my entire life that involved falling, drowning, and, worst of all, Nazis. The Nazis were always coming for me. I had a respite from the dreams the year I was with Joe, but now I knew they were coming for me, and there was nothing I could do to stop them. I thought that if I found a protector, a lover, a caretaker, they would be staved off, or at least I hoped they would be. I needed saving, but I didn't quite believe that I could be my savior.

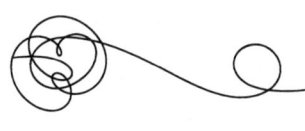

Cheap Date

I SAT IN MY GYNECOLOGIST'S OFFICE for my annual on an icy afternoon in February. I adored this woman, Dr. S. It took me years to find a physician that I could talk to and trust who didn't look at me like I was an idiot when I asked questions. My last lady doctor was a wretched man "in-network" who, when I described debilitating monthly bleeding, suggested I wear extra pads and get a hysterectomy. Dr. S was not only a terrific medical practitioner, but unlike every other doctor in New York State, she believed in limiting her patient load to get to know the vaginas she spent her days examining. I appreciated this immensely. She took a holistic approach to even an annual Pap smear, always asking me about the kids, my love life, and even my diet and sleeping patterns, taking extensive notes throughout our conversations. I actually looked forward to my visits with her, aside from the whole stirrup-and-speculum combo, though she was so thoughtful, she even warmed the metallic torture device up before its insertion.

I was flipping through a magazine when she came into the exam room, and we began our appointment, which was part friendship, part medical, and part therapy session. We started with the basics. She told me that it appeared I had lost weight since our last visit eight months ago. She was right. I had lost weight. When I am sick or upset, I can't eat. Food tastes like sawdust in my mouth and eating nauseates me. Since I had been both upset and sick each month since October, my eating had led to a long stretch of tiny meals that I choked down once or twice a day to keep me going.

She asked me how my love life was and even mentioned Joe by name. I told her he had ended the relationship but that he hadn't yet moved and that we still communicated daily. I shared with her that it was a rough couple of months, but I was starting to get back out there and that the process had been unpleasant. On the plus side, I told her that I was getting my appetite back, so I thought I was on the right track.

She put down my folder and the pen she took her copious notes with, peered out at me over her glasses, and said, "Rachel, what are you doing with this man? What is going on with you?"

It was a good question, and I answered her honestly, "I don't have the first clue, Dr. S. But isn't knowing that half the battle?"

She laughed. "You're almost fifty," she told me. "I understand this man hurt you, but you need to move on and away. I think this isn't about him at all. I think it's easier to focus on him than the other things on your mind."

This thought had never occurred to me. I had been so focused on either getting Joe back or meeting Joe 2.0 that I thought of little else.

She continued, "Besides, don't you think, at our age, relationships are overrated? It's not like you want to have children now, or get married again, do you? Why don't you have a little fun? You have worked hard all your life. You're raising your kids essentially by yourself and starting an exciting new career. Do you have time for a relationship? Do you even want one? Think about it. It's another person that you'll end up taking care of given your nature. When you want to have sex, take a lover. When you're done with him, move on."

At that moment, I understood that Dr. S was the greatest doctor who had ever doctored. I teared up right there on her table. *I'm going about things all wrong*, I thought. I thanked her profusely as I laid back for the exam. While she was inspecting my lady parts, we planned together. From that moment on, I would have fun and take this much less seriously. We decided I would try Feeld, the dating app that was fun and flirty, and enjoy myself for a change. Normally, when something appears in the *Times*, it is already passé, but in the case of this dating-app thing, I decided to give it a look-see. After all, my brilliant physician had vouched for it and even told me that if I liked it, she may try it herself. I left her office lighter than I'd felt in months. The next evening, I downloaded Feeld and started the familiar process of setting up my profile.

Almost immediately, I was inundated with attractive men who liked me. I'd heard that the algorithms on these apps do this when you first join to get you to subscribe at a higher level, so I decided to wait a week to see if the flow persisted before I committed to paying for the app. It held steady for a week as I quietly scrolled. By week three, the steady stream became a mighty river, so I broke down and subscribed. Feeld was described as open, honest, accepting, and sex-positive. Since my doctor's philosophy had taken root, I felt excited to meet new and interesting people. The men seemed smarter and more professional than on the other dating site I'd deleted. I wasn't sure who I should go out with first given the interesting conversations that I started with several men on the app, but I ended up meeting Ed.

Ed lived in Washington Heights, the same neighborhood where he was raised. He had one nine-year-old son, and though he was never married to the boy's mother, they remained close friends and coparented well together. He was a foot surgeon who

My Year of Really Bad Dates

also had a practice where he made house calls, mostly to the elderly residents from the Upper West Side to North Harlem. He graduated from high school early and began his college education at an Ivy League school at the age of seventeen. We met for a drink at Rudy's in Hell's Kitchen, one of the best dive bars in New York. In addition to a good atmosphere and a great patio, they also serve free hot dogs. They were fat and juicy-looking as they sizzled in an old-fashioned glass box complete with metal rollers. I was getting over yet another sinus infection and finishing up my antibiotics, which made me sick when mixed with alcohol and most foods, so I drank two seltzers with lime while he had a beer at four o'clock on a Tuesday afternoon.

I liked him. He wasn't my type physically, but he was smart, funny, and dedicated to both his patients and his son. I found him attractive based on his personality, wit, and intellect. He was also a little older than I would normally date, in his early sixties, but he didn't look or act his age. Besides, this was supposed to be the new fun, flirty me! I didn't need Mr. Right, or my usual judgments and tastes. I wanted to explore and see what was out there. We spent two hours together, and then he had to pick up his son from his karate class, and I had to catch my train home. He walked me to the train, which was great because it gave us more time together. He kissed me right there in front of the Thirty-Fourth Street entrance to Penn Station, and it was a very good kiss. I smiled as we parted ways, and we made plans to see one another again soon. I let him know that I was going to Florida for a quick consulting gig at a conference and was looking forward to seeing him when I returned.

I WENT DOWN TO PALM BEACH for the conference, a holdover from my old life as a professional Jewess and museum CEO. An old donor to the museum thought I could potentially be helpful

Cheap Date

to her on a new project, and I did find it interesting. Since she was hosting a small invitation-only working group, I decided to kill two birds with one stone and both attend the working group and look at the opportunity. While I was away, Ed texted daily. He was funny and warm and told me he had been thinking about me and looking forward to seeing me again.

Joe also texted while I was away. I told him I was in Palm Beach and that the resort was beautiful. I sent him a photo and he responded by telling me that maybe the next time, we could go together. He still had not made up his mind about whether he wanted to move to Phoenix. It was getting strange. To this day, I'm not sure which one of us was the bigger fool. I think it was me. Intellectually, I understood that my continued communication with a man who had left me for another woman was futile, but by this time, I was so deep into trying to get him to stay that I couldn't see the forest for the trees. I had been adrift for months and I still clung to the idea that he could save me. I had never been saved by anyone, and the idea that someone could or would even want to save me was intoxicating. I couldn't stop the high that I felt when I imagined what it would be like to open my front door and see Joe standing there, waiting to sweep me off my feet.

WHEN I GOT BACK TO NEW YORK, Ed and I decided to go on our second date. There was an exhibition on Mayan religion in art and sculpture that I had wanted to see at the Metropolitan Museum of Art, and he hadn't been there in a while either. We met at Penn Station right by the escalator and hopped on the subway to the East Side. It's a bit of a walk from the subway to the Met, but New Yorkers are walkers, and neither of us minded. The only issue was that the sleet that was pelting the streets when I left home had devolved into a torrential downpour. For a split second, I thought about suggesting we hail a cab, but I didn't want to appear precious even though I was dressed for a date with my favorite handbag and shoes not meant for a monsoon. I wanted to portray myself as a fun, flirty, casual gal. Fancy shoes? Cute purse? Pshaw! Who cared?

Ed was wearing the same outfit that he wore when we met at Rudy's, which I assumed was his work uniform. He spent his days bending down a lot to examine people's feet, and he needed to be comfortable, which is why he wore sweatpants and work shirts under his leather bomber jacket, which was well-worn. I noticed that the shoulder was torn and there were a few holes. It made me smile and reminded me of my ex-husband, who also wore clothing until it fell to pieces on his body. I always found this trait endearing and liked the fact that he was not a materialistic man.

The museum was mobbed, and he led me to the line where New York residents can buy discounted tickets for cash. He asked me if I had cash on me, but I told him I could do better. The rewards for working in museums for decades are few, but the one benefit is a card I have that gives me reciprocity at any museum in the world. I presented my card at the information desk along with my ID, and we were immediately given two free tickets. This thrilled him, and he told me that I could prove valuable, which made me laugh.

We walked through the exhibit together, talking the entire time. We shared stories about our lives and kids. He made me laugh and I thought it was going well. Around two in the afternoon, we decided we were each a little peckish, and I would need some coffee if I was going to make it through dinner with my mother and her boyfriend later. The Met offers a few different options for food. There is a beautiful restaurant downstairs in a courtyard that is a touch romantic. There is a café on the second floor that is more casual and overlooks the atrium, which is also

Cheap Date

lovely. He suggested the third option, a coffee cart that serves small sandwiches on the third floor. I was slightly disappointed, but I also understood that we didn't have a lot of time, and the service was always a bit slow at the first two choices. There are some folding tables and chairs next to the cart where you can sit and take a rest in between the floors. I got a coffee and a small sandwich; he got a cup and filled it with water at the fountain. He had eaten lunch early with a patient, he explained when I asked.

As we sat and sipped, he commented on my purse and asked me if I, like other women, had a "thing" for purses or shoes. He'd gotten me there. It wasn't judgmental, more a question that men wonder about, and a topic we'd discussed in text messages and in person as we strolled about the museum. We'd also explored the different values that men and women have in our age bracket. I confessed to him that I do have a little thing for handbags and that every other year or so, I buy myself one. I'm an experience-over-stuff person, but I do love a good designer bag, though I'm disciplined about my purchases. Out of the blue, he asked me how much the bag I was carrying cost. The question took me aback for a second, but it should not have. I have often been accused of being more Israeli than American due to my bluntness. I would think nothing of it if an Israeli asked me the same question. I even appreciated that he was so open about money given the fact that most men in my experience are terrified of the subject. Other than my father, who often bragged when he spent five dollars on a pair of pants at SYMS (a terrible discount clothing barn in Buffalo, New York, with enormous public dressing rooms and awful fluorescent lighting that held their sales in large bins with signs that screamed $10 OR LESS!!), the man I married and every man in his family quaked at the mention of money. I have never understood this panic. Perhaps it is the Jew in me, or growing up with relatives who would ask how much someone paid for a carpet, but I think talking about money shouldn't be taboo.

I told him that I'd spent $1,100 on the bag. It was the first that I'd purchased in about four years, the last being before the pandemic. He looked shocked but didn't say anything as he stared at the bag, turning it in his hands almost like he was giving it a medical exam. He then shared with me that he had just purchased a new lounger and showed me a picture of his adorable son sitting in the chair. In the photo, his son was surrounded by metal shelving and cardboard boxes, so I assumed the chair was in his office. He told me that it was his apartment and asked me if I'd like to see more photos of his place.

I scrolled through the photos on his phone. His apartment, which he told me he'd lived in for twenty-five years, looked like every college apartment I'd ever spent a drunken party night in between 1990 and 1995. There was an Iggy Pop poster on the wall. Not in a frame, mind you, but tacked onto the wall with pushpins. Each room was outfitted with metal shelving. His bedroom had not a single piece of furniture other than his bed—a wooden-framed futon. Instead of an actual coffee table in the living room, there were milk crates with a piece of plywood placed over the top. In another photo, his son was eating a slice of pizza off a paper plate, which he told me was easier and less expensive than washing dishes. He told me he could get one hundred paper plates for ninety-nine cents at the dollar store near his apartment.

I broke out into a cold sweat as a chill ran up my spine.

My father lived like a hobo for most of my childhood. He too had a homemade coffee table and for years slept on a mattress and box spring on the floor. I could never spend a night in any of his various fleabag apartments because, for years, he had no beds and no furniture. He owned two cups, two wine glasses,

Cheap Date

two bowls, two plates, and two place settings of silverware. The brown-and-white corduroy sofa he schlepped from apartment to apartment reeked of stale cigarettes, as did his hundreds of paperback books, which he kept on rickety wooden shelves that he insisted on putting together himself. Approximately once a month they would collapse, and he would curse and spend half a day putting them back together. Each time, another screw would be lost. Once he spent an afternoon "fixing" a door handle in his bathroom. It took him three hours, and when he was finished, the handle was upside down, so that when you opened it, you had to pull the lever up and to the right instead of straight down like every other door handle in the world. Ed's description of his home triggered me. I hate the word *triggered*, and I think it is often overused, but in this case, I was triggered hard.

I needed to validate if he was truly as ridiculous as he appeared, and I asked him why a doctor chose to live like a college student. "That is my aesthetic," he answered, smiling sweetly.

What aesthetic might that be? I wondered. If he was going for the look of a storeroom in the back of an Ace Hardware store, he'd nailed it perfectly. He told me he preferred to spend his money on travel and experiences over material possessions. This was a positive since I felt the same, and I asked him when he'd last traveled and where he went. He thought for a minute. It was a decade ago, and he'd gone to Florida for a long weekend.

We wrapped up our coffee klatch because it was getting late and I had to get a train home soon. As we exited the museum, we discovered that the torrential downpour had turned into a full-on blizzard with a delightful mixture of snow and sleet that felt like it was blowing through your soul. Ed told me that he thought we should get a cab back to Penn Station. I was relieved, and frozen, so he hailed a cab, and we hopped in the back seat together. As we drove through the gale, he turned to me and said,

My Year of Really Bad Dates

"Since you don't mind spending $1,000 on a purse, I'm going to have you pay for the cab."

Game over. I smiled and told him I would happily pay the fourteen dollars for the cab ride, which included the tip. I scanned the previous hours we had spent together. I'd provided free entry to the museum, paid for my coffee and sandwich, since he couldn't find his wallet, and had now paid for the cab ride. Come to think of it, I'd also paid his subway fare, since I was ahead of him when we went through the turnstile. I just handed my subway card back behind me the same as I do with my children when I take them into the city.

We arrived at Penn Station. He was taking the subway to pick up his son, and I was taking the train home to get ready for dinner with my mother. As we stood in Penn Station, I told him that I enjoyed our time together but I didn't think we were a good match. He seemed surprised and asked me why.

I told him that I didn't want to sound bougie but that while I'm not materialistic, I do enjoy dressing up now and then and dining in a restaurant where I don't have to shout my order into a clown's mouth. He smiled and told me I was not the first woman to tell him this but that he had no plans to change. He then snidely implied that the women of today are shallow and looking to take advantage of men financially and that I should find depth in dating instead of looking for a wallet.

I knew some women fit his description, but I assured him that I was not one of them. I wanted to date a grownup, not a wallet. I explained that I had worked hard in multiple jobs for decades. Now, I could occasionally enjoy a nice evening out, a pretty handbag, and a vacation once a year. I stopped halfway through my little speech. Why was I explaining myself to this man? Thankfully, the loudspeaker saved the day by calling the track number for my train. I wished him well and descended the

Cheap Date

stairs to find my seat. I was wet from the snow and sleet and exhausted. My beautiful shoes were saturated, and I was worried they wouldn't recover. I felt worthless, but I always felt that way on some level. My parents were not much for boosting my ego. Mostly, they were angry that I didn't do what they wanted or look how they thought I should look. My mother criticized me constantly, and my father's favorite thing to say, after describing something I'd just done, was "What kind of idiot does that?"

My needs were not important to my ex-husband. He couldn't meet them, but also, he didn't want to meet them because he needed so much. Not only was I responsible for meeting his and our children's needs, but I was also solely responsible for meeting my own. I mostly felt like I was doing a terrible job at all of it in general. I worked a hundred hours a week, and by the time I cooked, shuttled, took care of everyone else, and cleaned up, there was no more time or energy for myself. I went years, decades even, squashing my needs down until I didn't think I needed anything anymore . . . until I didn't think I should have needs or even that I deserved them. If nobody else cared about them, why should I?

I sighed thinking about how the dinner with my mother was not going to help my emotional state much. The last time I had dinner with them, my mother's boyfriend asked how my book was going. I told him it was out on submission, and he responded by whispering in my ear, "Don't hurt your mother!" The book, a memoir about my life with my father, was in their minds somehow about her. It's always about her.

I wondered briefly as the train pulled away if I should return to therapy, but I quickly dismissed the idea. I had been in therapy off and on for years, with only one great therapist all that time, and the fatigue and haze in which I was wandering at that point in my life made me think that therapy wouldn't help me. Nobody could help me, I thought. I felt both helpless and not deserving of help, because if nobody had ever helped me before, why in the world would anybody care enough to now? I had fantasies about being saved, about being a damsel rescued from a tower, even though I hated Disney princesses and anything that implied that a woman needed saving. Suddenly, however, I needed a lifeline and couldn't figure out how to grab it or where it would come from. I wanted to be my own rescuer, but on some level, I also knew I wasn't up for the job.

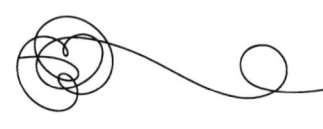

The Wallet

JONATHAN HIT ME UP ON Feeld toward the end of February. He was handsome in a distinguished kind of way, with salt-and-pepper hair and a terrific smile. We exchanged some banter online, and he was smart and witty, not to mention incredibly active from the looks of his profile pictures showcasing himself in front of a small plane, riding a horse, and parasailing. He looked like he belonged on the cover of *AARP: The Magazine*, and I told him so, which made him laugh. His age was not listed specifically, only that he was over fifty, which was fine by me. His profile indicated that he had three grown children, and I pegged him for about fifty-six, or maybe fifty-eight. He was at the top end of the age range I usually go out with, but that was okay too.

After a few weeks of texting and a couple of late-night phone chats, we decided to vibe check over a coffee. The vibe check is the most basic form of dating math. When you two-thirds like someone, have a daughter in tech week for her play that keeps her at school for sixteen extra hours over five days, and have a son with three put-together dance rehearsals for four hours at a stretch to prepare for the first dance competition of the season, that leaves approximately fifty-four minutes to grab a quick coffee that week to see if you like the guy enough to go on a proper date.

Jonathan and I met at Rockefeller Plaza, and for a minute, I watched the ice skaters in front of the big tree and relished

My Year of Really Bad Dates

being in New York. It was always such a fun time of year to be in the city, and I realized how lucky I was to live here. We were meeting at a seriously good coffee shop, although it was a chain. They made a chicory coffee just like in New Orleans, and I was glad Jonathan loved it too. The shop was in the basement of 30 Rockefeller Plaza, or, as it is more popularly known, 30 Rock, and I had never been to this specific location before. I couldn't find the place and I texted him. He was lost too, but he asked for directions and guided me over the phone, joking that he was my Seeing Eye date, leading me to caffeine heaven. I laughed as I saw him on the phone talking to me, and we both hung up at the same time and hugged. It was a nice hug. A good hugger is just as important as a good kisser, so this was positive.

The coffee shop was crowded, and he suggested we get our drinks to go and sit on the comfy couches in the lobby of the building. It was a great idea, and we did it, sitting side by side at an easy angle while we sipped and chatted. I was wearing a shortish skirt and cute tights, so he got a look at my legs. He noticed and complimented them, and not in a lecherous way, which I appreciated. He was very upfront about his age from the get-go, informing me he was sixty-five years old. I was shocked. He didn't look his age in the least. I've gone on dates with men in their mid-forties who looked like they were sixty, and I told him he looked great. This seemed to please him, and he told me that he wanted to be very open about this because he could understand if this would give me pause.

It did.

However, I liked his energy, and once the cat was out of the bag about his age, our conversation was fluid and easy. We had similar backgrounds, similar interests, and similar outlooks on life and love. He was Jewish, and his father was a Holocaust Survivor. He wasn't religious and only identified culturally, but he was

The Wallet

certainly proud of his heritage. I never cared what kind of religious background someone had when I considered dating them, but I thought it might be nice to date someone Jewish for a change. The fifty-four-minute vibe check lasted ninety minutes, and we were both late for our next appointments when we reluctantly parted ways. What impressed me most was his old-school gentlemanly goodbye. It was a nice warm hug and a sweet peck on the lips. There was no tongue ramming, no feel copping, and no weirdness. It was so refreshing that he grasped the concept of time. We had nothing but time to get to know one another. We texted back and forth, and he invited me out to dinner the following week.

JOE, ALWAYS LOOMING LARGE and still sending me good-morning text messages like when we were dating, asked me to coffee that Sunday afternoon relatively close to my house. We laughed a lot and were genuinely happy to see one another, but the talk turned, as it always did, to his Phoenix plans. I found myself getting upset, and as I did in the rare moments when we were together, I started to cry. Again. I hate crying in public places, and he knew this about me, but I couldn't help myself. He told me that seeing me vulnerable was like getting to know me all over again, and he liked me that way. He was not the first man to say that about me. I remember once when I was spending an afternoon on a boyfriend's sofa watching old movies, I started to cry at a tender moment in the film. When I returned from retrieving tissue from his bathroom, he was staring at me.

"Why are you looking at me that way?" I asked him.

"Sorry, I just never saw you do that before. It's like you're a real person."

My entire life, I wanted more than anything to be vulnerable, but there was never a space for me to express that emotion

My Year of Really Bad Dates

or to cry. My parents constantly referred to me as Sarah Bernhardt whenever I cried, rolling their eyes and telling me everything was fine. If I ever expressed any emotion at work, and by *emotion*, I mean clearly and passionately describing something that I thought was a terrific project or a truly awful one, I was told I was dramatic and needed to "tone it down." My ex-husband always wanted to have sex with me after he saw me cry and would tell me he found me irresistible when I was vulnerable. The irony of course was that while he liked to see me vulnerable sexually, he had no interest in helping me maintain emotions or meeting any of my needs. When I told my in-laws I was very scared that I would have to commit my new husband to an institution and that I would have to do it with no health insurance, I was told that I was a "drama queen" and that "lots of people are without health insurance; you're fine." I tried to live like Sheryl Sandberg, but every time I leaned in, I fell over and onto my face.

Joe wanted me to be vulnerable and emotional but strong and independent. He didn't want to rescue damsels anymore, or so he said, but here he was, attracted to his ex-girlfriend silently weeping in a coffee shop. All I wanted was to be held and for someone to tell me it was okay, but Joe couldn't do it, and I couldn't do it for myself.

ON THE DAY OF OUR DATE, Jonathan texted and asked me if I wouldn't mind coming to his place first and going to dinner downstairs in his building. He had a business call that would likely go a little late, and he was apologetic. This is not unusual in New York City, as a lot of buildings have commercial spaces on the bottom and residences on top. I told him it wasn't a problem and headed over to Hudson Yards.

The Wallet

Hudson Yards was opened in 2019 on the West Side of Manhattan between Chelsea and Hell's Kitchen. In addition to the most luxurious residences in the city, it boasts the highest-end mall in New York and an obscene, ugly bronze structure in the center that can be climbed. As far as I can tell, its sole purpose for existence is for people to Instagram themselves in front of it or on top of it or to use it as their dating-profile photo. The only place that beats it for social media and dating-profile pictures is Machu Picchu. The wealth in the building borders on the grotesque, and it is home to New York's 1 percenters. It is rumored that with your purchase of the apartment, you are guaranteed space in the Billionaire Bunker, a structure beneath the ground that apparently will withstand both the zombie and nuclear apocalypse. The über-rich can ride out the misery in style while the rest of the peasants burn.

This guy had money. A lot of money. So. Much. Money.

He was unassuming on the phone and in person, and I never thought that money, either having none of it or all of it, should be a factor in whom you date. I dressed nicely in case he wanted to go to one of the luxury restaurants in the mall attached to his apartment, and I was looking forward to meeting him on his turf. The apartment was beautiful, the view astonishing. The palette was neutral and lovely. He had great taste in furniture and decent taste in art. We chatted about this and that as he finished up some paperwork. I looked at his photographs of his children and his grandchildren. There was a picture of him in front of the plane I saw on his dating profile, which, as it turned out, was his very own. He told me it was in the shop and bemoaned the fact that it was always in the shop. He then laughed about how bougie and ridiculous he sounded, which made me like him even more. We went out to a casual dinner in a gorgeous restaurant in the building. Another perk of living there is that there is always a table for a resident, so no reservations are required.

My Year of Really Bad Dates

After dinner, I went back up to his place with him to get my bag and he kissed me. It was nice and I liked the way his arms felt around me. He asked me if I wanted to spend next weekend at his house in the vineyard. He wanted to take me flying in his plane, and this was the perfect destination for our next date. I was flattered, but it felt a bit too soon for me to commit to a weekend, so I asked him if I could think about it, and he seemed taken aback. I told him that I really liked him and enjoyed our two dates, but I just needed a day or two to think about a whole weekend.

The last weekend away I'd had with a man was for Joe's birthday the previous May. I took him upstate to a converted monastery. We ate a lot and took long walks and hikes, but we also spent the majority of the weekend in bed. It was incredibly relaxing, and we had a terrific time. At one point, late at night when we were cuddled up and he was kissing my neck, I almost told him I loved him, but I stopped myself. What if it was just the weekend talking? What if he didn't say it back? I had not told a man I loved him in years, whereas Joe, historically, fell in love at the drop of a hat. Within two weeks of meeting a woman, he was telling her he loved her and was in a committed relationship. I always found that weird and red flaggy with him, especially when he described the train wrecks that he'd dated throughout his life. When he told me his history, I explained very early on, on date three, that I was not that kind of girl. At the time of this birthday trip, we had been together for about five months. I wanted to tell him I loved him, and I did love him, but my fear stopped me. He felt the same way. I wasn't the kind of girl he usually dated: basic, insecure, and jealous. He wasn't the man I usually dated: messy, intellectual, and distant. We were both just insecure idiots even though, on a lot of levels, we were finally doing the whole dating thing right.

The Wallet

I WENT HOME AFTER THE DATE with Jonathan and did some reconnaissance. When you have worked in the Jewish philanthropic world as long as I have, it is not hard to find out about a Jew in New York. We are, after all, a cabal that controls not only the space lasers, banks, and entertainment industry but also information about our fellow tribesmen. After two phone calls, I got some background information. He was, as I thought, a decent guy who had a raw deal in his marriage and had dated a lot of women. The friend of a friend who gave me the information told me he was surprised that he was dating me since he never dated Jewish women. It was interesting information but not something that would have swayed me either way.

There was one other thing that gave me pause about the weekend away, which was the tiny plane that he would pilot. I am not a scaredy-cat about most things. I have a very high tolerance for risk. However, I hate small planes. Because of my work, I have had to take a lot of planes all over the world alone, and as I have aged, I have become deeply disenchanted with airline travel even on a gigantic plane with an upstairs. But tiny planes are the worst. Even the cute name of "puddle jumper" does nothing to assuage my irrational fear of a tiny plane with me strapped into a seat, crashing into the ocean. I'm not a rock star or an heiress or a daredevil movie actor, so I'm certain on a logical level that I won't die in a plane crash, but the unnatural fear still exists. Everyone has at least one stupid fear, be it spiders or earthquakes or snakes. Tinyplaneophobia is mine. I didn't want to tell him this since I like to save most of my neuroses for date five or six, but over coffee the next day, I broke down and told him anyway, since I was trying to be more vulnerable in relationships. He laughed and told me that was exactly the reason I should go with him for the weekend. He wasn't wrong. But the more interesting truth was that I loved the last man I spent the weekend with, and I wasn't sure I was ready to let anyone see me for that length of time yet, nor was I ready for the feelings that might be conjured over a three-day period.

We had another nice date and a make-out session, and I was surprised by how attracted I was to him because he wasn't my usual type, but I decided to buck that. I was now fun and flirty and having a great time! After some thought, I decided to go with him to the vineyard. The odds of me dying in his plane were about as low as me being chosen as *Sports Illustrated*'s next cover girl for the swimsuit edition. I was glad his plane was in the shop since it gave me time to think and decide based on comfort level as opposed to a time crunch. We met a few more times while he waited for a part that had been held up in the supply chain issues that were still a reality after COVID. There were nighttime phone calls in between our dates. He talked about his daughter and how he was trying to help her start up a new business. I told him about my kids and the challenges of reinventing myself while raising them essentially alone.

Finally, the part came in and was successfully installed, and he asked me to meet him for a drink so we could plan what I had come to think of as "The Big Weekend." I was looking forward to it, and I headed out on a cold day to Hudson Yards for coffee in his apartment. I was starting to feel comfortable around him. It was a nice slow pace we were taking, and I found myself melting into the relationship like the big square ice cubes in a good old-fashioned.

And then, it happened.

We sat down at the island in his kitchen over steaming cups of coffee and he suddenly got a serious look on his face. I asked him what was wrong, and he took my hand and told me he had

The Wallet

been meaning to talk to me about something important, which he referred to as the "elephant in the room." I didn't realize there were any animals in the room, let alone a giant zoo animal, so I asked him what was up and reassured him he could always be honest with me.

"I like you, Rachel. A lot. I think we could have a real future, though I know the age difference has given us both pause."

I smiled, relieved that this was the ten-ton animal to which he was referring. When I started to tell him I was okay with the difference, he shook his head. In addition to the elephant, there was more big game in the room. This one was an angry hippo.

"I just need you to understand that I can't support you financially."

I stared at him, confused.

"I'm not sure what you mean here, Jonathan." I was hoping he'd had a ministroke or had confused me with someone else.

"Don't get me wrong," he told me reassuringly. "I'm happy to pay when we are together. I wouldn't even mind taking you shopping now and again. It's just that I'm overcommitted financially with my own business and children, and it just wouldn't be right. Besides, don't you think you'd feel better accomplishing your own financial goals?"

I gaped at him. I had already achieved most of my financial goals. On our dates and on the phone and over text, we'd talked about all kinds of things, but we'd never discussed money, since he was supposed to be my date, not my financial advisor. I already had one of those and he'd always done a terrific job. Jonathan knew nothing about this aspect of my life. I was proud of what I'd accomplished in my professional life and the freedoms that work had given me financially and in lots of other ways. He had not been to my house, and while it wasn't an ivory tower, it wasn't a shanty either. I adored where I lived, and I wouldn't

My Year of Really Bad Dates

have wanted to live in Hudson Yards for love or money. I had never asked the time of day from a clock, but this man, whom I'd known for barely a month, decided that I was an aging sugar baby, looking for an aging sugar daddy to take me to a mall and buy me a pair of designer jeans. What was I, fifteen?

I tried to calm myself down because his implication had infuriated me. I was sure that some women were out to use him as a wallet, but I was not one of them. Trigger alert once again, despite my hatred of the phrase. For decades, my in-laws, their family members, and even a few of their friends would snidely imply that I had "expectations" of them, which roughly translated into: *You were a gold-digging whore out to take us for everything we have to better your trashy self.* The irony of course is that if I were a gold digger, my license for the practice would have been revoked. There was no gold. I knew there was never going to be any gold. I married a character actor with a depressive disorder. I was pretty sure from the get-go that there would be no gold, and I was fine with that.

In the twenty-five years I was with my ex-husband, I was often accused of trying to take his family's cash. His wealthy father and stepmother gave us money twice. Once my ex-husband promptly squandered the sum by purchasing an apartment in Chicago during a major depressive episode without telling me most of the details. The second time, we borrowed $17,000 after I was laid off and he had quit his first nine-to-five job in the throes of another depressive cycle three years later. He had quit his job without telling me and started day-trading, also without telling me. I had just given birth to our son, and after decades of working one hundred hours a week, I had asked him if I could take two years off to be with our baby and toddler. Then, I promised, I would happily go back to work. My off time lasted less than eighteen months. Within three weeks I had a six-figure job

The Wallet

as vice president of the Olmsted Parks Conservancy in Buffalo, New York, though after a year, I was laid off. In the ensuing years, I twice saved up the money to repay them, but each time, there was an emergency, again engendered by a depressive cycle.

The actual gold digger in the relationship turned out to be the white man born into incredible privilege who lived off my back, not the Jewish girl born to a public-school-teacher mother and a gangster father in the most blue-collar city in America. I loved my ex-husband dearly, and he had and has many positive attributes, but earning a living was never one of them.

The double standard between men and women when it comes to dating that bothers me most isn't sex, power, education level, or geography. It is money. Middle-aged women, especially single mothers, are automatically assumed to be destitute, trying to trap themselves a man to buy a house or a car or to better their station in life. Inexplicably, women in my age group have bought into this hook, line, and sinker. Most middle-aged men view themselves as the great financial hope for us scraping and desperate creatures. If women are so terrible with money, and never expected to have any, then why is it that so many women I know are now the family breadwinners? There is another supposition that men make, which is that divorced women have all taken their exes for a ride financially. I have a friend whose ex-husband went after her future earnings because she got her real estate license, which she paid for, while they were married. I know a man who left his wife and put all his money, which he had been hiding from her, in his girlfriend's name to avoid paying child support, which was crazy since she made more than he did.

I was the breadwinner for twenty-two years, working insane hours while he rode his bicycle, played a patient diagnosed with an assigned disease at an osteopath college for twenty dollars an hour, and did some small-time theater with his friends. Oh, and he had lots of time to himself. Despite my supporting him for decades, my ex-husband wanted and collected alimony for a year. When my father died, I gave him every nickel my dad had in the bank, about $40K, because I knew he needed it to get an apartment and get his life together. He has never paid a penny in child support. Yet, the narrative in his universe and among his people remains that I forced him to marry me, made all the decisions, and left him penniless when my evil money machinations were not met.

I WAS SO DEEPLY OFFENDED by Jonathan's statement and how he presented the "problem" to me that it took me a few minutes to recover. Once I had taken a few deep breaths, I very slowly told him that even if he offered to take care of me financially, I would refuse even if I needed it, which I did not. I would also not take expensive gifts until and unless we had established a long-term, committed relationship. Additionally, I explained that I would never want to go shopping with him or any other man I'd been dating. When I do go shopping, which is roughly two to three times annually, I go with one man, my friend Josh, who picks what he knows I will like. I'm in and out in an hour because, on a good day, I have the patience of a tsetse fly.

Rather than appear apologetic, Jonathan came across in his response as patronizing. He smiled, tilted his head to the side, and told me he just wanted to make sure I understood the ground rules and that he would spoil me "now and then." *Now and then? I thought. Like when I've been a good girl and get an ice cream cone?*

I stood up and told him that I wouldn't be able to fly off with him after all because I couldn't see him anymore. He smiled and told me that was why he was always upfront about the situation at the start of the relationship. He thought I was leaving because

The Wallet

he wouldn't pay for my life. I told him I was leaving because he didn't respect me enough to think that I could do it myself. For a brief minute, he looked like he might apologize, but it was as if he couldn't fathom what he had heard and wouldn't have believed me anyway.

As I left his apartment, I was still fuming, and the tears came. I felt humiliated that a man I didn't know well could make me feel this way. I went back through our conversations in my mind to try to see if I'd ever given him the idea that I was looking for him to support me. It made me think about the perception versus the reality of my marriage. I spent twenty-two years banging my head into a wall trying to prove to my in-laws that I was not a lying, manipulative, gold-digging idiot. No matter how much I loved my husband and children, no matter how many jobs I took on to make sure they all had what they needed, and no matter how many times I alone nursed my ex-husband through deeply dangerous depressive episodes, I could never shake their story about me. After being told by my parents that everything was always my fault, and having that sentiment reinforced in the male-dominated universe I chose to pursue professionally, I internalized it all. The bad stuff, as they say, is often easier to believe than the good stuff, and after years of being told the problem was me, I believed the external voices. I was the problem. But I could be better! I truly believed that if I worked harder, they would see who I was: smart, competent, honest, and loving. I was sure they would see that side of me with enough work. I was sure they would all see.

They never saw.

As I boarded the train home, I remembered something my ex-husband told me when I asked him why he never confronted his family or said anything to them about the way we were treated. He shook his head and told me that nothing would have changed how they thought about either of us. I always thought it was his lackadaisical attitude, or that he had simply been beaten down by decades of emotional abuse and gaslighting. I saw it as a weakness. However, at that moment, I saw clearly that he was 100 percent right. He had been much smarter than me in this context, and he never had to bang his head and get frustrated. In the end, some people will always believe what they want. If his family had acknowledged that my ex-husband and I were decent, honest people who were just struggling with serious mental illness, that would have forced them to look in a mirror and ask themselves why we were anathema. They didn't want to do that, and I understood why; they were too far into the story. If they stopped to see who we were, they may have had to pause and lend a hand, and nobody wanted to do that for us. Making us the bad guys made their lives easier.

I did some math in my head, not dating math but regular math. The amount of time that I had wasted trying to prove a negative was tremendous. Years of my life, and decisions I'd made, all in the name of proving I was not something, instead of proving that I was someone. The tears came again, and I wasn't able to stop them as the train rolled on. My sole consolation was that Jonathan would never be able to really love anyone if he saw every woman as being out to take him. I won't ever own a plane, but I think I can see people for who they are, not what they want or have. If I end up alone, it will be because I just didn't find my person, or because I chose not to have a partner, not because I couldn't trust a potential mate. No number of facts or amount of evidence can sway a person committed to their belief system or the programs that were instilled in them by parents, society, religion, or anything else that imprints on the human psyche.

My grandmother was right: People who marry for money deserve every penny of it, and I'm glad I didn't.

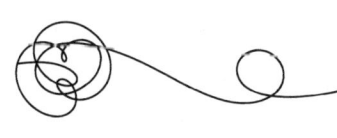

The Hamster Wheel to Nowhere

IT WAS THE END OF FEBRUARY, and I was crying alone in my car after lunch with Joe. He'd invited me, and I was hopeful that he'd decided to stay in New York. But instead he told me he was leaving. Definitely. For the third time. It was truly over, and though logically I'd known that it was over from the first night back in September, I still harbored the childish fantasy, in some part fueled by Joe, that he would sweep me back off my feet and declare his undying love for me. Now, I knew it in my gut that he was leaving. That he was always going to leave.

Additionally, Joe shared with me that the home he bought in Phoenix had been purchased jointly with his blond real estate agent. This was a key piece of information he had been withholding from me since November. She couldn't afford a house on her own, and it became clear to me that she knew he could. I felt the relationship was transactional, and I told him so. On some level, Joe understood this. He kept telling me it wasn't a choice between me and her. It was a choice between being near his aging parents and the rest of his family or me, and he repeated that sentiment over the lunch he paid for but I couldn't eat since I felt like I was going to throw up. He was going to marry her and live in mediocrity ever after in a median-price house in Mesa, Arizona, and I was a fool who would die alone with a cat I hated who hated me back. I didn't want to cry in front of him again, though he looked like he was also choking back tears. We hugged it out in the street to say our final goodbye to one another.

"I'm sorry, Rachel. You're amazing. I only want the best things for you. You know that, right?"

I held it together while I walked to my car, refusing to look back even though I knew he was watching me walk away. I waited until I had driven a few miles before I pulled over to weep uncontrollably. While I cried, I thought about every failure in every relationship I'd ever had. It was like watching a bad Lifetime movie on a loop in my head without the good lighting and terrible music. I felt I was destined to live life alone; in that moment, I felt like the least desirable woman on the planet. Every terrible thing that had ever been said to me, or that I had heard about me, was roaring in my head, and I believed every word.

My college boyfriend, Karl, flashed before my eyes. He was six years my senior and had already graduated from college when I started dating him toward the end of my sophomore year. He was the big man on campus and was president of Stage Troupe, the largest student organization at BU, which put on plays and musicals by students who were not theater majors. The parties were legendary and the drugs and alcohol plentiful. To me, he seemed impossibly clever and grown. He had his apartment and car, all of which were subsidized by his wealthy parents while he drank copious amounts of Wild Turkey and made smart remarks.

Two years into the relationship, when I was a senior in college, he moved to Los Angeles to break into the entertainment business but spent most of that time smoking Camels on the couch his parents bought for him. As soon as I graduated, I too moved to Los Angeles and got a job. I had no desire to be in the movie business, but I had no desire to do anything else either. My mother had sold my childhood home to live with the most boring

The Hamster Wheel to Nowhere

man I had ever met, and my father was married to a mentally ill drug addict who hated me, and the feeling was mutual. Even if I had wanted to go home, it was not an option. I was alone, confused, and terrified, and I clung to the relationship with Karl like a baby chimp clings to its mama.

The relationship had been awful from the start. But it got much worse. By the time I moved to Los Angeles, he had stopped having sex with me. He told me I was overweight and not smart. He treated me like I was a child. He was emotionally abusive and cruel to me. I stayed because I was living alone in a strange city for the first time, and like the child I was, playacting in adulthood, I believed that if I was smarter, thinner, more sophisticated, or prettier, the relationship would improve, since, of course, the problems were all my fault. This warped idea followed and plagued me for decades, setting up the rest of my life in every relationship, both business and romantic, that I'd ever entered. Any problems in these relationships were my fault, and any success was attributed to dumb luck.

I lost an extreme amount of weight. I began to color my hair and change its style. Pictures of me from the time show that I was unhealthy and sickly-looking, but even after the doctor told me not to lose any more weight because I was going to make myself sick, nothing changed. Karl even went so far as to tell me that losing weight emphasized some of my "less attractive" features. I couldn't win for trying. And I still tried.

I was working in international sales for a film company and was making good money, which he spent. We finally broke up when he left me at a party to have sex with another woman, who happened to be the crush of one of his closest friends. When I told him, two months later, that I had started to date the man I would go on to marry, he slapped me across the face, shoved me out the door, and slammed it on my foot, breaking two of

My Year of Really Bad Dates

my little toes. He was friendly with my future husband and saw our relationship as a violation of what he referred to as the "bro code." Many years later, after I was married, we bumped into each other at a party, and he apologized profusely and begged my forgiveness, which I gave. After that, we mostly traded jokes and barbs on Facebook.

He died last year of cirrhosis after decades of abusing alcohol. I cried in my car for him, though I doubt he ever shed a tear for me. I cried in my car for the years I could have had fun dating college boys but spent devoted to him. I cried in my car for what wasn't, isn't, and never could become with my ex-husband. I cried because I wasn't worth it to Joe and was convinced, at that moment, I'd never be worth it to anyone else. I'd never cried as much in my life as I had in the six months since Joe left me in September. It was almost March and things were not getting better, but much worse. I couldn't sleep, and I could barely eat. I was frozen in my writing as I waited for my novel on submission to be picked up. It was not picked up. I wrote thirty thousand words of a great idea, but the writing was so awful that my brilliant editor Emily asked me if I was okay since this was not like me to send her such a mess. A song on the radio could move me to tears. I had to pull over into the parking lot of the local grocery store when Phil Collins's "Against All Odds" came over *'80s on 8* because I became almost hysterical.

By March, every day felt the same, like an unfunny *Groundhog Day*. I was only able to focus on my failures since everything negative or terrible that ever happened to me was clearly my fault. I wasn't sure what rock bottom was for me emotionally, but crying over a dead man I hadn't dated in thirty years in my car alone on a side street of a shitty Long Island suburb seemed close.

When I got home, my ex-husband was there, eating the last slice of the cake I'd made the day before. The kids weren't

The Hamster Wheel to Nowhere

supposed to be home as it was his one day of the week to spend with his children. I had been hopeful that I could go home, finish up my cry, and get ready for the date that I had stupidly scheduled for that evening, but there they all were. What a fool I was to believe that I had a right to be alone in my own home on the one night a week I was legally released from responsibility for my children. I asked them why they were all congregated in my living room, and my son told me that he had a headache and just wanted to take a nap in his own bed. I asked why he couldn't take a nap at his father's apartment.

My ex-husband just shrugged as he swallowed the last piece of blood orange cake with a sweet glaze that I was planning to eat while I cried. Did I mention it was the last piece? I said nothing. Instead, I did what I had been trained to do for the entirety of my life by my parents, my husband, his family, and the men I worked for throughout my career: I shoved the abuse, grief, rejection, and sadness down to absolve the perpetrators and make them comfortable until I didn't have feelings or care about anything. I am the expert when it comes to squashing my feelings. There isn't a feeling in the whole wide world that I can't stuff down into my feet and sit on for a year or two while I wait for a convenient time for everyone else to be ready for me to express it. The problem was that it was never convenient for me to have an emotional moment or a breakdown. Those moments were reserved for everyone else in my life. Even when I expressed my hurt casually, I was told that I should not feel that way, or that I was a manipulative drama queen, or, my personal favorite, told to me time and again by my ex-husband's family: *Get over it.*

I wanted to get over it, but first I had to figure out what the "it" was specifically that I needed to get over. I swallowed hard—the pain in my throat was fantastic—cracked a joke, and went upstairs to hide out in my room and get ready for my date.

My Year of Really Bad Dates

As I made my way upstairs, my ex-husband said, "You look tired. You should try to get some more sleep."

I *was* tired, and I'd been crying in my car for an hour, but I didn't appreciate him pointing out how hideous I looked. At the time, he was dating a thirty-three-year-old girl with breasts that would make Dolly Parton envious. I bet she never looked tired. When I was thirty-three, I had a year-old baby and was working a full-time job and doing consulting work on the side. I wonder if I looked more tired back then or now.

"Gee, thanks. I appreciate you telling me how shitty I look."

"Jeez, don't be dramatic. I'm not being critical . . . I'm just concerned for you. Forget it."

"Thanks again. Where were you when we were married? You didn't seem too concerned when I was exhausted then."

I wanted to scream and cry and tell him that I was a mess and I desperately needed help, just a little help now and then, but I didn't. I just swallowed hard again against the giant lump, managing to hold back a fresh round of tears for a change (swallowing them was getting harder with each passing day), and headed up. I had to get ready for a really bad date after all, and there didn't seem to be enough energy in reserve to both straighten my hair and have an emotional outburst.

THE DATE WAS AT WHAT was described online as an upscale pub in a strip mall. I arrived to find my Sir Galahad for the evening wearing a porkpie hat and a Members Only jacket that looked like the one my father owned in the late seventies. I was already put off. It wasn't just the jacket, though that should have been reason enough for doubt. I don't think anyone whose name isn't Corey and who isn't starring in an eighties rom-com or teen film about prom night should be wearing a porkpie

The Hamster Wheel to Nowhere

hat. It was his whole vibe. He was pacing like a panther outside the bar.

When I approached, he said, "Hey, I don't think this place is good for a first date. The light is bad, there are only candles everywhere, and some guitar trio is playing. But I noticed a place a few stores up that looks great. Do you mind if we go there?"

Dim lighting and romantic classical music to create an ambiance would be a date killer for sure.

We headed to the Asian restaurant a few stores over because he seemed deeply uncomfortable, and I was happy to go along. The restaurant was flooded with fluorescent lighting so bright that it could be used as a lighthouse for boats sailing through the Long Island Sound. The hostess seated us in an enormous booth that could easily have fit ten people. I could not understand why she had done this, since the restaurant was empty, but then I saw her wink at my date, and I knew that this had been prearranged. I wasn't sure from which planet this man came that made him believe a cavernous empty restaurant with a huge banner across the lobby that read ALL THE CRAB YOU CAN EAT SUNDAY was preferable to woo me, but I settled in for sixty minutes of hopefully decent dumplings and perhaps some good conversation.

I was disappointed on both fronts. He spent the bulk of the evening interviewing me as though he were hosting a beauty pageant. It is nice when a man takes an interest in his date, but it gets less nice when he conducts himself like he is interrogating a prisoner in Guantanamo. He asked me question after question, but they were all questions that would never get to the core of who I was. He asked me my favorite color. Had I ever watched *Seinfeld*? He wanted to know what kind of car I drove and told me that he could tell a lot about a woman by her car. This surprised me. I leased my car, the first new one I had ever driven, because I went to a dozen dealers, and the one I chose was the best deal.

My Year of Really Bad Dates

What insight could he glean from this information other than the obvious, which is that Jews don't pay retail? Joe, Mr. I Love Mustangs, used to tease me all the time that I drove an old lady's car. I could have been home in bed crying and watching reruns of *The Mary Tyler Moore Show*, which airs on MeTV on Saturday nights. Instead, I found myself the guest star on the most boring *Barbara Walters Special* ever produced in a cheesy restaurant that was lit like the sun.

I tried to ask him questions about himself, but he answered each with one syllable. Even when I used every technique in my arsenal as a trained oral historian, I could not get him to give me more than three words about himself at a time. The conversation lagged quickly, but luckily, the food arrived. Sometimes, a good meal can spark conversation and make a dull date passable, though chewing tinfoil and shaving my head with a cheese grater sometimes seemed more appealing than a boring first date.

Sadly, the food was as dull as the conversation. My date, drooling over his General Tso's chicken, finally admitted that it was his favorite restaurant, which made me wonder why he went through the subterfuge of suggesting we meet at the pub a few doors down.

Digging in, he said, "This place is great because they make food the way normal people like it, you know? Not with all those weird spices. And they use a lot of good sauce, which makes it more authentic, don't you think?"

I was no expert in Asian cuisine. But I have been to China and Thailand in Southeast Asia, and the food was very different and much more flavorful. He seemed shocked that I had traveled to Asia. "Ugh, you went all the way there? Why? I hate traveling. Besides, I'd never go to Asia because they are so anti-American."

I was not sure what he meant by his statement, though I had a good idea. Over dinner, he asked me where I had been over

The Hamster Wheel to Nowhere

the last five years. I was pretty sure Europe, Central America, and Israel were not currently at war with America over any issue unless I missed something, but he still gave me side-eye.

This brings me to yet another fun dating topic: the Trumpers who Make America Grotesque Again. Most men seem to understand, at least on some base level, that broadcasting to smart, successful, decent women that they want to make America great again cuts their pool of prospective pussy by half or more. Instead of checking off the box labeled "conservative," which is a dead giveaway, they list themselves as "moderate" or their political beliefs as "other." This could mean many things: Libertarian, Independent, Communist, Rigel VII supporters; it really doesn't matter to me as long as they do not support a man who lies when he breathes, eroded trust in our institutions, incited an insurrection that killed four cops, has been found liable for sexual abuse, and uses tanning cream to obtain his nuclear-orange hue. And those are only the attributes that crest the top of the list.

I find it annoying when men lie about their political bend on a dating app for two reasons. One, it shows they prioritize getting laid over their own convictions and principles, which I find reprehensible. Two, it wastes time better spent watching reruns of *The Bob Newhart Show*, working on my latest book, hanging out with my kids, or clipping my toenails. Before you tell me that I should ask up front, you should know that online dating is awkward enough without expecting a dossier of the person's voting history and political leanings, especially when they identify themselves as the opposite of what I'm looking for. It's already weeded out in my settings, but now, I am expected to play detective to discern if my potential date is a fascist. How should I do that over text? *Hey, you seem great. I've enjoyed chatting so far, but before we go any further, can I please have your voting history for the last ten years? Asking for a friend.*

My Year of Really Bad Dates

But back to the really bad date at hand.

I wasn't sure how South Asian people could be construed as anti-American, but I didn't see a point in keeping the conversation going. It was only going to lead to nowhere and end with him mansplaining to me about research, deep states, and conspiracy theories about President Biden's relatives.

The meal came to its merciful and inevitable conclusion. The good news was that he clearly understood that he was as uninteresting to me as I was to him, and that ensured no awkward moment as we parted company, never to see one another again. However, he did leave me with a parting statement: "You should do some research about Asia. They really hate America. Most of the countries you seemed to travel to hate America."

I just nodded and turned away after our goodbye and good-luck handshake.

He got into his car and left. I went into the pub where we were supposed to meet since it was Saturday and I felt like a glass of wine. The place was fantastic, the atmosphere delightfully mellow, and the guitar trio, which was playing classic flamenco beautifully at the perfect decibel level, might have been the best live music act I'd seen in a year. I ordered a pinot noir at the bar and had the privilege of listening to three marvelous musicians perform two numbers, including a rendition of "Entre dos aguas" that moved me to tears. When they finished, everyone in the bar applauded thunderously.

The middle guitar player was fine as hell. He strolled up to the bar, and the bartender handed him a drink. He sat down next to me, and I told him that I thought he was fabulous. We struck up a conversation, and he was slick. Cute—and slick. I had not gone out with a ponytail-wearing guitar player since college, but for this guy, I was willing to make an exception. We had a great conversation for over half an hour until our drinks were drunk,

The Hamster Wheel to Nowhere

and I realized it was getting late and I had to get home. He asked me for my phone number, and as I was about to give it to him, a woman sidled up behind him, draped her arms around his neck, and told him they needed to get going to pay the babysitter. He smiled at me and shrugged, which I found incredible. It's a bold move to hit on a woman in a bar where your wife, the mother of your children, has come to support you and watch you perform. If it wasn't so sociopathic, it would have been hilarious. I thanked the bartender and slipped out as his poor beleaguered wife planted a kiss on him. It was like watching my puggle pee on something to mark his territory. I wanted to put my arms around her and tell her to run for her life, but I resisted the urge and drove home.

The date was a bust, but by the time I pulled into my driveway, the evening was chalked into the win column. I may not have met Mr. Right, and the date was yet another on the wheel, but the music was heavenly, and I got a great story. The melody found something inside me that I thought was lost. While most music made me cry during that time, in that one moment, it felt restorative. It was the power of art reflected in my mess that made me feel like a real live woman again.

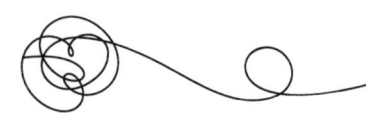

The Luck of the Irish

CONNOR COULD HAVE HAD POTENTIAL. A lot of potential. The second I sat down at the Algonquin Bar in Midtown I felt a spark. He was tall, Irish, sexy ugly (think Sean Penn or Harvey Keitel), and there was something slightly off about him that I couldn't quite place. I sensed he was emotionally ruined inside, like most of the men I have fallen madly in love with throughout my life. He was also hilarious and brilliant and had a prestigious intellectual job. Our first date was a series of zingers, banter, and trading books we thought the other should read. We loved the same kind of music and both of us felt as though we should have been born in a different time. It lasted three hours and we reluctantly parted company since he had a book party to attend, and I had a dinner date.

I had stupidly stacked my day to have drinks and dinner, two first dates, since I was spending the day and night in the city. I wished I hadn't. I was annoyed at myself because if I hadn't, I suspected he would have invited me to the book party, which sounded endlessly fascinating as opposed to this date, a fix-up from a friend of a friend. But Connor and I promised to see one another again soon.

The dinner date was about what I expected. He lived in Jersey and had a lot of money, which I only knew because he told me. Multiple times. Over and over. He let me know that in his

The Luck of the Irish

divorce, he paid his ex-wife $5 million. He used the word *mill* instead of *million* because he wanted me to know he was generous and humble. He even lowered his voice when he said "five mill" lest the busboy or waiter know how much money he had and expect a large tip. Dating math told me that when he said she got five mill, that meant $2 million, including the family home.

He returned his voice to normal volume to share the gem that his ex-wife was a "narcissistic twat," which in my opinion negated his generosity. If I were him, I would have lowered my voice to lay that statement on a first date, but that's just me. I asked him why it was that so many men become psychiatric clinicians in the process and aftermath of divorce. It seemed to me that on several dates, men had used phrases just like that one to describe the women they once married and chose to be the mother of their children. Other popular diagnoses for ex-wives include: bipolar, sociopathic, psychotic, manic, borderline, and the overarching vague label of mentally ill. He laughed and proceeded to tell me that in his extensive dating experience, most women were one of those things after they go through menopause.

This made me sigh out loud. My ex-husband spent years telling our two children that I was crazy because I was going through menopause. When we first split up, he called several of my friends to let them know that I was crazy and going through menopause. That was almost five years ago, and I have yet to skip a period. Months before fifty, I remained as regular as a clock. My doctor even warned me to be careful when I had my IUD removed because despite my age, pregnancy was still logistically possible. I wish I was going through menopause. It would make aspects of my life much easier, but alas, I still have a few miles to go before I arrive in HRT town.

As much as I enjoyed a good chuckle at the provincial sexism displayed by certain entitled, unfunny, privileged white men

My Year of Really Bad Dates

who were probably shitty husbands to begin with, that night, I found it extra annoying. I thought about Connor and how much I would rather have hung out with him in the pouring rain than endure this blowhard in the trendy Upper East Side eatery he had chosen. When the date was over and I was on my way home, Connor texted to tell me that he wished I had gone with him to the party because it was frightfully dull, and I was exceptionally beautiful. I texted back:

#swoonworthy.

The next afternoon, I was writing in my girlfriend's apartment when Connor texted to ask me what I was doing. I explained that my friend was away with her family and had offered me the use of her Upper West Side apartment while she was gone. It's a great apartment, very quiet, and a great place to write undisturbed. I told him that I would be delighted to see him and to come on up so we could grab a coffee.

The second he stepped inside the front door, he was on top of me, kissing me like a man who had just been released from a solitary confinement prison term of fifty years. It was like I wasn't even there as he groped me and licked me. It felt like a cat giving me a tongue bath. I was afraid. How could I have been so stupid? I barely knew this man, and I'd invited him up to an apartment I didn't live in during the day, when no neighbors were home. I pushed him away and asked him to calm down and stop, and to my great relief, he did. He sat down on the sofa and put his head in his hands. During my career, I interviewed thousands of Holocaust Survivors. I can spot trauma a mile and a half away. I cautiously sat beside him and asked him if he was all right. He was not all right. I knew there was something off with him, but I was way off base when I was contemplating the possibilities.

Connor had been diagnosed with terminal cancer several years prior. His health had seesawed over the years, and he'd

The Luck of the Irish

moved to the United States primarily for health care. He explained that an experimental drug had saved his life and put his cancer into remission. Our first date was the first date he had gone on in years. Only a few months ago, his doctor suggested he get back out into the dating world because he had a future. He didn't think it was fair to date a woman if he was going to die on her. He'd had to give up the woman he wanted to marry and the idea of having children. He apologized profusely for his aggression, but he liked me and was very attracted to me and got carried away.

My heart went out to this man. I wished I could be half as vulnerable as he had just been with me. His naked honesty made me like him even more. I told him that we had nothing but time and that I was as attracted to him as he was to me. He had tickets to a concert in two weeks at a famed New York club and asked me if I wanted to go. I immediately accepted. We had a coffee and shared a nice kiss before he went back to work.

I HAD BEEN IN FAIRLY frequent touch with Joe via text, but it was mostly pleasantries and a little bit of me telling him he was insane for leaving New York. I had also taken to texting him the phrase

Fuck You

. . . after every bad date or unpleasant experience. The joke was that since he left, everything rotten that happened to me was his fault.

In a stunning turn of events, Joe called me out of the blue at the end of March.

"Are you okay?" I asked. I was worried someone in his family might have died or something.

"Yeah, I know. Listen. I was talking to my boss's wife today. What am I doing? You're amazing. I have been at this job for thirty-two years. I can't leave all this behind. I'm calling to tell you I changed my mind. I love you. I want to be with you."

I almost fainted. After all the months of heartache, he wanted to choose me. I missed him still and the idea of being chosen was so intoxicating, the logical part of my brain put up a Gone Fishing sign, and the little girl desperate to be chosen by any man ever took over the entirety of my cerebral cortex. His condo was sold, and once the closing date was set and he was packed up, he wanted to move in with me and the kids, likely late spring. He told me he could not compare me to his blond real estate agent because there was no comparison since she was so far beneath me and his feelings for me. He had a meeting that night, but we decided to get together the next night so we could talk it all out and begin to plan our future. I was elated and not sure if I should tell anyone about this reversal or if I should just keep the good news to myself, but when my kids got home, I wanted to tell them that I thought perhaps Joe and I would get back together. They liked him, and I wanted them to know, but I decided to wait so we could tell them together. I spent the evening clearing out a few shelves in my closet to make space for him so I could show him that I meant business and that I was making room for him in both my heart and my favorite physical space in my home.

My ex-husband came over to drop something off the next morning. He walked into the house, as was his way, without knocking. He asked me how things were and if it was a good time to talk about college applications. Our daughter was applying to theater schools. Despite my best efforts, she wanted to follow in her father's, grandfather's, and great-grandfather's footsteps and be an actor. As a parent, I always thought my child was the prettiest and most talented child ever to grace the earth, but I never knew if that was through the rose-colored glass that all mothers

The Luck of the Irish

see their children through or if she had a real gift. He assured me that she was gifted and told me that he would be unable to contribute to her education financially. I was unnerved by this statement. My ex-husband, an Ivy League–educated man with a master's degree that I paid for, never had any money. This was the case even though I absolved him from child support and every penny he earned went directly to himself. He proceeded to tell me he would approach his fabulously wealthy father to see if he had started a college fund for his grandchildren and if he would possibly contribute something.

As nice as that would have been, I wanted *him* to pay for it. I wanted *him* to take care of things. I wanted *him* to fulfill one commitment that he made to me, that every other normal married man with children has committed to fulfilling. It almost wasn't about the money but about the validation that we once were a family and that families are supposed to share the load. It was not his father's responsibility (we learned soon after that there had been no fund set up by either of his parents) but ours— his and mine together. I started to explain all of this to him, but he begged off, telling me he had to get back to work. However, before he left, he had one more nugget to share. He was going to Barcelona with his thirty-three-year-old girlfriend over spring break. In our twenty-five years together, he took me away overnight once, for my fortieth birthday, though my best friend set it up for him. He told me at one point that traveling made him uncomfortable, and that if I wanted to travel, I should find a companion to go with because he would not accompany me.

It amazed me that I could still get emotional over my ex-husband's behavior. I did not miss him as a partner because he wasn't a good one, but the fact that he was making the effort to be a real live boyfriend for a thirty-three-year-old girl stung. It felt like a betrayal of my work, my love, and my needs that he always refused to fulfill. It made me feel like I was one inch tall and worthless. I had nothing left inside to give to anyone, let alone myself, so I kept looking externally since I felt so empty within.

The college fund my father started for my kids now resides in the hands of the woman with whom he spent the last twenty years of his life. The legal reasons continue to confound me, but in a nutshell, he put her name on the account because he also had started an account for her grandchildren, and therefore, the money belonged to her. I begged her to only take what he had set aside for her grandchildren and leave the rest for my kids, but she refused. I had never been able to put much into the account I started because we were always broke, and I was always taking on extra side work just to sustain us throughout the marriage. The tears started to fall, but I brushed them away because Joe wanted me. Together, we would be something incredible.

An hour later, Joe texted to ask if I was free to chat, so I called him.

"Hey, baby! Are we ordering sushi for dinner tonight? Do you want me to pick it up on my way to your place?"

"Rachel, I'm so sorry, but I made a mistake. I gave my notice at work today. I'm leaving for sure. I have to go. I don't know what I was thinking yesterday. I guess I just panicked. I'm sorry."

I was in shock, which quickly turned to anger and then rage. I don't remember what I said to him exactly, but the gist was that he was the worst person whom I had ever met and I hung up on him. I felt like the biggest idiot on planet Earth, and for a minute, I wondered if I was dead. I couldn't move and I collapsed in a heap on my kitchen floor, which was where my children discovered me hours later when they got home from school, just to round out a perfectly awful afternoon. I was ruined. He did not choose me after all. *Nobody chooses me or will ever choose me*, I thought. I was the unchosen of the chosen people. In my world,

The Luck of the Irish

it never rained men, only shoes, and on that fateful Tuesday, it was a downpour of spiked heels.

Against my better judgment, and because I couldn't sleep, I wrote Joe an email to let him know how really awful I thought he was and how he'd demolished me. I had hung up too quickly before I could tell him what I thought of him. I expected never to hear from him again, but he emailed back the following day to tell me he felt wretched, couldn't sleep, and was terrified to let go of me. He implied he made another mistake and didn't want me out of his life. He told me again that his blond real estate agent couldn't compare to me in any way and that on many levels, he knew that letting me go could be the biggest mistake he would ever make. I should have let go and let God, my ex-husband's favorite twelve-step phrase, but it was becoming clear that I was addicted to the idea that Joe would come back to me.

I finally broke down and called my girlfriend to tell her the latest. I had not shared most of the Joe saga with anyone. In part, this was because I understood my behavior was ludicrous and I was ashamed of myself. I also knew that my friends were disgusted with Joe and were sick of me pining for a man they thought was beneath me. I chose the right girlfriend to talk to because she very gently told me that it was clear to her that I was addicted to this cycle and that I should break it immediately. She was of course right. And yet, I couldn't seem to walk away, and neither could he, even though he was involved with another woman and planning to live with her in the house they had purchased together.

In between crying, I hazily agreed to chaperone my daughter's cast party, which should speak to how low my defenses had gone. As my daughter went on later that week to point out in her senior speech on closing night of her starring in her last high school musical: "My mom even agreed to chaperone the cast party, which she hasn't done since my third-grade farm trip."

My Year of Really Bad Dates

The agony had almost made me forget, but my date with Connor loomed large despite my zombielike state. We texted daily, and sometimes he called me. His intellect was intoxicating. If date three was half as good as our first two encounters, I would be thrilled. Maybe then I would be strong enough to finally "get over" all the things that people have been telling me to get over for years. I would be able to tell Joe to kick rocks. I would regain a shred of my confidence and self-esteem. I would be done with the shoe storm. I already had enough heels, flats, boots, and slippers to last three lifetimes that had fallen on my head for years, and perhaps the sky would finally clear.

I STARTED TO FEEL POORLY on Saturday afternoon. I had been sick monthly since October, and it drove me crazy. I have always been an awful patient, and I have no patience for even my illnesses. The New York winter was unusually mild, which was great for the snow-averse but terrible for those Ashkenazi Jews like me who are cursed with wretched sinuses. I had a headache for months, and I was losing weight because all my food tasted like mucus. I might have been sick because I was barely eating and blowing my nose fourteen times an hour. I also wondered if I had a terminal disease. I called my doctor, who told me it was likely the effects of the antibiotic that she'd given me a few weeks ago, and if I didn't feel better by Tuesday morning, I should call back and come in for a checkup. I called Connor to tell him I was a little off, and if he was nervous that I would get him sick, he should take someone else to the concert. He was adamant that I meet him and hear this musician live.

Despite how I felt on the inside, as I looked in the mirror on my way out, I was surprised at how good I looked. Joe picked that exact moment to text and ask me how I was doing. I sent him a

The Luck of the Irish

photo as a response, and he told me I looked incredible, which pleased me though I wished I didn't care what he thought.

The concert was every bit as impressive as promised. We listened, we drank, we laughed, and at one point he even took my hand and patted it sweetly. After the show, we strolled through the village just as the rain stopped, and it was one of those magical New York nights after a storm. The streets were glistening, the lights were glittering, and only the most dedicated New Yorker was out and about on a Monday night. We stopped at a little bistro that was quiet and romantic and had a drink and a late-night snack. The banter, once again, was on point, and he told me about his upcoming trip that he had been looking forward to for months. We parted company and he went in for the kiss, which I stopped. If I was coming down with something, I certainly didn't want him to catch it and ruin his plans. He simply laughed and told me I looked too pretty to be sick. He went in for a deep and passionate kiss, and I kissed back just as passionately. I drove home with a smile on my face.

BY THE MORNING, HOWEVER, my throat was on fire. I couldn't stop coughing and I felt like hammered shit. I called the doctor, and she suggested I come in and get swabbed for yet another infection. Her nurse came out to the car first, stuck a Q-tip up my nose so far that it massaged my brain, and then did it again, telling me that the doctor wanted to run a full viral panel since I was sick so often. Once Nurse Ratched was finished, Dr. E, whom I adore, came out and told me to go home, get into bed, and force liquids while she ran the panels. She thought it was still the lingering sinus infection but told me she wanted to be sure. If I didn't hear from her, I should assume that all was well and that I would feel better in a few days. If anything came back positive, she would let me know. Wednesday came and went with little relief, and in fact, I felt worse. Thursday afternoon, I got the call. Dr. E told me I had COVID-19, but what was worse, I had something else she called human metapneumovirus.

"Well," I joked with her, "at least it isn't animal metapneumovirus, and I won't bay at the moon."

She did not laugh in response, and I took this as a bad sign. I could usually make her laugh.

I was put on a series of drugs. She was nervous that I would end up in the hospital since my immune system was obliterated. She told me I was highly contagious and couldn't leave my bedroom unmasked. She also put the fear of God into me regarding the whole metahardtopronounce thing and told me that when someone contracts it with another virus, they often end up hospitalized. I called my ex-husband, who picked up the drugs but refused to take the kids overnight because he didn't want to get himself sick.

I sighed. It was always like this throughout our life together, so why should I have been surprised that it continued in our non-together life? When I was pregnant, he refused to do what all expectant fathers do for their enormous wives. He wouldn't run out to get me ice cream or offer to do the grocery shopping so I wouldn't have to lift heavy things. It made me sad, but there was never time to be sad. Before I got pregnant with our daughter, I miscarried three times and had a misdiagnosed ectopic pregnancy that left me twenty minutes away from bleeding to death. I lost my left fallopian tube along with the baby. Nobody in my husband's family, to this day, has ever mentioned it or checked in to see how I was feeling after the surgery that saved my life. I spent the nine months I was pregnant with our daughter panic-stricken that I would lose her, but nobody else seemed to notice my state of mind because my husband told me

The Luck of the Irish

that everything was fine. They all kept telling me I had nothing to worry about. I was a "drama queen" and "neurotic."

With time and space, I now see that any normal woman in my position would have the same thoughts and that my feelings at that time were legitimate. But never mind those. After all, I had to pay for his graduate education, and he got his degree shortly after she was born. To afford it, I taught night school through UCLA extension classes and took on side work writing grants while I worked to get a land-use permit to build a permanent Holocaust Museum in Los Angeles. I was nine months and two weeks pregnant when the Parks Commission in the State of California permitted us. I went into labor the following day.

In the end, my ex-husband finally agreed to take the kids for one night, but only because I told him that Dr. E strongly recommended that they not be at home. I would likely become sicker before I got better, and Paxlovid had a myriad of rough side effects. I immediately called Connor to break the news to him and encourage him to get tested. I felt terrible that he was exposed to my sick mess, and I was deeply apologetic out of the gate.

Whatever apology I made did not quench his fury.

"You're kidding me," he said.

"I know. I'm so sorry. I had no idea I had even been exposed. My doctor suspected it was the holdover from—" But I didn't have the opportunity to continue.

"Fuck. I need to go get tested now. If I can't make my trip, I will be furious."

"I know. I'm so sor—"

"You know, this was fucking irresponsible of you."

"I know. Again, I had no—"

"Forget it, I just can't deal with you or this right now. It was ridiculous of you."

My Year of Really Bad Dates

I sputtered in embarrassment. I was humiliated, but at the same time, I remembered that I had tried to let him know I wasn't feeling well, but he wanted to see me. I decided to gingerly point that out. His icy response indicated that was an error in judgment.

"I can't talk to you. I'm going to urgent care." Then he abruptly hung up on me.

I was sick as a dog and crying in my bed. Joe chose that moment to check in on me, and I texted him through my tears what had just happened. He was outraged on my behalf. I wanted to keep texting with him, but I was about to be violently ill. Joe, very wisely, told me to stop fighting the nausea and let it all go, so to speak. I spent the next hour throwing up everything I had ever eaten.

The next ten days were a blur of Kleenex, tea, saltines, and electronically moving money onto my kids' cards to order dinners. I missed my best friend from childhood's fiftieth birthday party, and that devastated me since I pride myself on always being there for my ride or dies. My incredible family of friends dropped off food in shifts and checked in on my kids. Friends from far away had milkshakes sent to my house through Door-Dash. My son, wearing a mask and gloves, brought me trays of soup, and my daughter did her laundry, which made me wonder if I was dying and nobody wanted to tell me.

I watched more television in ten days than I'd watched in the previous year, including the entire *Game of Thrones* series. I had fever-filled dreams: my father telling me that I screwed up this time, my ex-husband throwing dirt on me, my friends having a party and wondering why I didn't show up, and Joe, leading me by the hand through a wood in the rain and showing me a bush under which I could take shelter. I dreamed about my grandmother's kitchen and the player piano in the mud room of our

The Luck of the Irish

neighbors' house where we kids used to sing "Bad, Bad Leroy Brown" and the score from *Annie* until their mother, Moira, would tell us to shut up. Joe checked in on me every day, but my ex-husband didn't ask once how I was, only texting regarding the kids. I felt connected to Joe, like he cared, and that maybe we still had a chance, though it was probably the fever causing that hallucination.

On day ten I started to feel human again. I took a step outside my front door and walked the dog around the block. I even sat at my desk for an hour or so and tried to write and return some emails before exhaustion hit. I tested negative for everything on the afternoon of day eleven and soaked in a hot bath until I pruned.

On day twelve Connor texted me:

I'm back from a great trip! We must get together soon.

The text confused me. I hadn't heard from him since he'd hung up on me angrily almost two weeks earlier. I wasn't sure whether I should respond, so I sat on it for a few hours until I finally wrote back:

Welcome back. I'm surprised to hear from you given our last communication.

Now, it was his turn to be surprised.

Really? To what are you referring?

His superior intellect belied his faulty memory. He implied he had no idea what I was talking about. I let him know that he was harsh in our last conversation and that he upset me when I was already in a fragile state, especially because I had enjoyed our time together immensely. He shrugged it off, telling me he didn't remember our last chat because he was getting ready to leave on his trip, but that he was looking forward to our next get-together. I wasn't sure what to make of the situation. Maybe he had that disease where the sufferer has no short-term memory, like the lead character in the movie *Memento*. Should I give him the benefit of the doubt and assume his angry outburst was a glitch? I'd ignored red flags before in relationships, and that never ended well. Was this a flag or merely a paper napkin fluttering in the breeze? His final text cinched the innate selfishness of his character when he wrote:

Don't worry about me, by the way. Nothing happened, I'm healthy and all is well. Never got sick.

Ah! He *did* have a memory of our last conversation after all. Certainly, I was glad that he didn't catch my too-hard-to-pronounce virus or COVID, but the fact remained that I was sick as a dog, and not once did he ask me about my state of health. I didn't respond and deleted his contact. On some level, he must have realized that I was done because he didn't try to reach out again. The Irish turned out not to be lucky for me after all. Bummer. I liked him, or at least the idea of him and who he presented himself to be and was not. Still looking externally, I wondered if Joe would finally pull his head out of his rear and figure out how worthy I was. The problem was, I was the one who didn't believe I was worth much or anything at all.

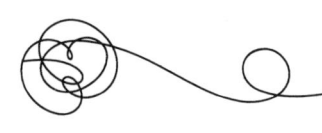

Dating in the New Age

JOE AND I CONTINUED OUR DANCE via text, though I knew that it was terrible for me. I knew he was leaving imminently, and a part of me couldn't wait for him to be gone. I stupidly thought that Joe leaving New York and living across the country would be the balm I needed to move on. And yet, I was afraid of how I would feel when he finally left. In truth, I was starting to unravel on all levels.

Still looking for a shred of self-worth, I continued to troll the most recent dating app I had joined. I was monogamous with my dating apps, choosing only one at a time. Late one afternoon, I was hit up by Evan. He was my age and the best-looking man I had ever seen on a dating app by a mile. He might have been the hottest guy I'd ever seen in general. If he was as good-looking in person, I would have been shocked. I couldn't believe it was even his real profile photo. After chatting lightly for a few days, suddenly, on a rare night when the kids were not at home, he reached out through the app and let me know that he was at his family home in my little beach town.

This isn't rare where I live. I'm on a barrier island a mere forty-five minutes from Midtown Manhattan, and a lot of people have weekend or vacation houses here. Some families have been here for a few generations now, and the fact that he told

My Year of Really Bad Dates

me his "family" vacation home was in Atlantic Beach meant he came from money. I often refer to my town as the poor man's Hamptons. If someone doesn't want to spend $10 million on a piece of land with a shack on it but still wants a beach house, my city by the sea is the place where people from blue-collar to super wealthy can live near open water. I have never cared about money vis-à-vis relationships or men or anyone, but I did like that he could pay his bills. I just don't like men who think I can't. I also had no interest in spending the next twenty-two years supporting a man like I'd spent the last two decades doing, nor did I want a man who calculates the precise dollar amount of my sweater and only eats off paper plates in his own home. Evan seemed to tick the money box for himself very nicely.

We had been messaging about being spontaneous in our lives, and since he was a mere two miles from me, he suggested that we meet at the diner down the street from my house. It was eight thirty on a rainy night, but he was right. We should all be a little more spontaneous in this life, and the kids were not due home until much later that evening. I decided to throw caution to the wind and meet him since it was down the block from me, and I could walk. And did I mention his profile photo? So good that I wanted to at least say I had gone on a date with a supermodel. There was a dearth of attractive men in my life at that time, and I missed that kind of excitement and energy. *Who knows*, I thought. Perhaps it could even be a wonderful date and the beginning of the end of my dry spell. I was essentially living like a Jewish nun, and I have never done well with celibacy. The truth is, I love sex. I crave intimacy and attention when it is with someone that I'm into, and when it isn't a part of my life, I can feel its absence. I had not had sex since the unfortunate episode with the below-average spaetzle, which seemed a lifetime and an ocean of tears ago.

Dating in the New Age

I walked down the block looking as cute as I possibly could on a rainy Tuesday night to the nearly empty diner and took a booth toward the back. Of course, the minute I sat down, my son's friend waved frantically at me from across the restaurant. She was eating a late dinner with her parents, whom I also knew well. Fantastic. I knew that within thirty seconds of my meeting Evan, she would take a photo and send it to my son. I pulled out my phone to suggest we have coffee elsewhere, but before I could type one letter, Evan glided into the diner. Dear lord, he was not as good-looking as his picture. He was better looking. By a country mile. He was six feet three inches at least and had long honey-colored hair, which was piled up in a man-bun on his head. Normally, this is a full-stop no-no for me, but this dude pulled it off with aplomb. He was wearing a Grateful Dead long-sleeved T-shirt, an old concert one with the bears splashed across it, another normally appalling feature for a grown man, but again, he managed to wear it casually without looking like a complete loser trapped in his college dorm room. For sure he followed the Dead by the looks of him, but I was willing to overlook that this once.

He smiled at me with the sexiest grin I'd ever seen as he slid into the booth across from me, after giving me a light peck on the lips. Holy hell he was hot. I resisted the urge both to drool and to tell him he was stunning. Instead, I told him what a good idea it was that we had been spontaneous and met on the fly. Again, he smiled at me.

"Well, I'm glad I got you while I can! You are beautiful and won't last long in this crazy online-dating madness."

Wow, he ticked every box. I blushed like a twelve-year-old schoolgirl. I may have even giggled. We both ordered herbal tea and laughed at that, as though it was hilarious that two grown people would order tea at eight thirty on a rainy weekday night.

My Year of Really Bad Dates

I asked him how long he had been coming to my little corner of the world.

As it turned out, he came from insane wealth. He was a competitive surfer in his younger years and had been all over the world. He never had what he described as a "traditional" job but, rather, had spent his fifty-one years on earth "studying culture."

"Culture?" I asked him. "Like an anthropologist?"

He seemed confused and asked me what an anthropologist was and does. I tried to explain the concept of anthropology, but I got a little lost halfway through our conversation because he took my hand in his. I missed holding hands with a man, even being lightly touched by a man. It had been months and more months. I loved holding Joe's hand. I used to fall asleep curled up in his arms with my fingers intertwined through his. Evan's hands were big and soft like he'd never lifted more than the weight of a surfboard in his life. He was holding my hand and stroking it, the way I used to with Joe after I'd been dating him for a couple of months. It was so intimate and intense that I found it a bit jarring.

He stared deeply into my eyes and I trailed off as he lowered both his head and his voice and said to me, "I always know when I meet someone I've met in a previous life, and you and I have met throughout time."

This was a revelation to me on a variety of fronts. In the first place, I'd remember a guy this hot through one hundred lifetimes even if I was a kumquat that he ate in his previous life. Second, I am not a believer in such things. I'm not saying there isn't something to the concepts of dharma, karma, and reincarnation. These things would never have survived throughout the ages if wise sages had not preached the concepts for thousands of years. I simply didn't believe that they applied directly to me at this moment on this date with this man.

Dating in the New Age

I laughed nervously and withdrew my hand slightly after giving his thumb a quick rub back. I used sipping my tea as the excuse to pull back lest he think I was a complete prude, but I was very uncomfortable. My mind was emphatically saying no, but my body was telling me to keep my big trap shut for once and perhaps experience what it would be like to date and have sex with the Adonis sitting across from me.

I smiled and said the only thing I could, which was, "Tell me more."

I hated myself for feigning interest, but the rational side of me was temporarily kidnapped, tied up, and locked in a closet by my libido and id. He smiled even wider and started talking to me using all kinds of New Age terminology that sounded like a word salad to me. The more he spoke, the dumber he sounded. It became apparent to me that he not only sounded dumb but that he was, in fact, dumb. As I listened to him talk about regression and the money he had spent, a decent fortune it would seem, on shamans, fortune tellers, and gurus as a "seeker of truth," I was more certain by the minute that he was not just dumb but the dangerous kind of dumb. The dumb where he truly believes he is smart. He told me his body was a road map to his spiritual journey, with tattoos of each trip and profound out-of-body experiences he'd drifted through over the five decades he was alive. I'm sure he revealed much more, but I was too preoccupied with how hot he was to pay attention, especially since he didn't seem to have the insight that not all of us were still in the age of Aquarius.

"How many tattoos do you have, Rachel?"

"Oh, me? Um. None. I never felt like I wanted something permanent on my body, I guess."

Evan was surprised that I did not have tattoos. It was more like shock, as though I had just told him I never put on deodorant or wore clothing. I started to explain that I was raised in an observant Jewish household and that would not have gone over well. I also told him that I wasn't permitted to pierce my ears until I went to college and was eighteen.

This news sent him over the edge, and he yelled out, loudly, "*No way!*" He shook his head in disbelief. "I'm Jewish too, but I've never heard of that!"

Now it was my turn to be shocked. I'd never met a Jew like Evan. A New York Jew who seems to know nothing about Jews. It was like seeing a dog walk on its hind legs or your doctor buying Metamucil or picking up a personal prescription of penicillin at the grocery store. It just didn't register as feasible. He told me that he had a great feeling about me and that he believed that soon he would take me to get my first tattoo. If he hadn't been so hot, I would have gulped my tea and made my way home. But he *was* so hot. I hadn't had sex in what felt like a long time. I hadn't had good sex in seven months. I was terribly lonely for the feeling of a man's arms around me. Besides, I reasoned, beauty was pain, right? I could nod and smile for a man this sexy, couldn't I?

As I turned the possibility over in my mind, he started talking about crystals, his latest passion, and the powers of crystal healing. He told me his next jaunt would be to Costa Rica, where he was planning on spending several weeks getting certified in crystal healing with the world's authority on the subject. He told me it would cost a whopping $25,000. I sputtered and came dangerously close to doing a spit take with the lukewarm tea in my mouth.

"Wow, that's . . . a lot of money," I said.

He rolled his eyes and told me money was a trip that he had never been into. I supposed that was because he never had to earn any. I laughed inwardly for a moment trying to imagine how the conversation would go with my father if I told him I was going to

Dating in the New Age

spend $25,000 of his money on a fake certificate in crystal healing. I couldn't think through the conversation, however, because I was quite certain that the aneurysm he would have after he heard the price tag would have killed him instantly. I wondered how Ed the medical professional—the man who wouldn't pay for the taxi, the sandwich, or anything—would have reacted to a woman telling him she was going to spend $25,000 on crystal healing. I wondered if Mr. I Can't Support You would have nodded and smiled if I had told him I was a crystal healer.

I made one last-ditch effort to make it work. I thought that if he had a sense of humor, I could overlook the rest and at least sleep with him once or twice.

"What does that certification process look like, and how do you add it to your CV?" I joked, trying to look sexy.

"What's a CV?"

"Oh, um, curriculum vitae? It's just a fancy word for a résumé."

He snorted and said, "Jesus, who even has one of those these days?"

Just then, my phone's telltale text ding went off. It was my son, and his message was clear:

You cannot date anyone with a man-bun!!! It's not allowed!!! You're embarrassing me!!!! Go home immediately.

I was on a date with an American Jewish swami nowhere near him and he was the one who was embarrassed? As I suspected, my son's friend had texted a photo that she had taken of me and the star of the local community theater's production of *Hair*. We finished our tea and headed out of the diner.

"Well, I have an empty house. Want to come back with me and see how we connect elsewhere?" His smile was incredibly sexy. I wanted to throw caution to the wind and screw his brains out.

But I couldn't.

My Year of Really Bad Dates

No matter how gorgeous he was, I couldn't get over the fact that he was going to spend $25,000 to look at rocks and get certified in something that was not a thing. Try as I might, I just couldn't do it. I hugged him and wished him good luck but told him I didn't think I was a good match for him. He looked sad. I was sad. I told him he would be a great fit for the right woman, but that woman wasn't me.

As I walked home in the cold, I grew progressively sadder. Why couldn't I just relax and go with things more? Why was I so judgmental? Maybe crystals and swamis and aura buffing are real and I'm just a cynical old spinster who will spend her golden years cleaning out litter boxes for cats that hate me. By the time I got home, I'd worked myself into a lather. Of course, this was the moment that Joe chose to text me to let me know that his condo had sold for an even better profit than he thought. The fucking jerk. I was angry at myself and couldn't believe I was still communicating with the man who'd demolished me. I wanted to stop but I couldn't seem to stop. Joe was the only person I knew who could turn a terrible life choice into a financial windfall. I responded the only way I could:

Fuck you. Now, if you could only pocket that money and live with me, all would be well.

But would all be well? I did miss Joe. I missed lying next to him and talking to him and the life I thought we would have together. But what was inside of me was starting to feel bigger. The brokenness I felt wasn't about a man, or a job, or my current life, or my old life, but rather all of it and none of it. I was crying constantly by then, over nothing sometimes. In the parking lot of Trader Joe's, an older man lit a cigarette, and as I walked by, the odor of the smoke and his aftershave was mixed with the sweet smell coming from the bakery in the same plaza. It smelled like my father, and I started to cry as I handed the cart off to the confused teenager waiting for it by the door.

Dating in the New Age

Late one night when I couldn't sleep, I was flipping through the channels, and on PBS, Sir Peter Hall's bizarre film interpretation of *A Midsummer Night's Dream* leaped onto the screen as the mechanicals performed their play. It made me weep as I remembered how proud I was when my ex-husband played Francis Flute, the bellows-mender, at the Ahmanson Theatre in Los Angeles right around the time we moved in together. I even got emotional when I was cleaning the kitchen and saw a half-drunk can of seltzer, my son's most annoying habit, and thought about the days, not so far off, when he wouldn't be at home where I could scold him anymore. I was starting to wonder, *If the clock was turned back and everything was exactly as it was last summer, would things still not be right?* That was the most frightening thought of all. What if I was having a nervous breakdown? Where were these emotions that were leaking out left and right coming from? I'd been the champ of shoving them down or pretending they didn't exist, but now, I couldn't stop any feeling from bubbling up. After a lifetime of feeling nothing, I was starting to feel everything, everywhere, all at once. It was at best unnerving and at worst some sign that I was going to end up in a locked ward somewhere scribbling my lunacy onto circular pieces of paper. I vowed to take a long break from dating then and there.

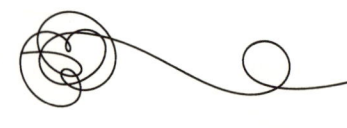

Short People Got No Reason

THE THING IS, I ONLY DATE MEN that are at least my height. I prefer taller than me, but five feet nine inches is the shortest man I will date. I realize I am a heightist and that I am excluding a huge swath of the male population, but this is a preference that was created long ago. That neuropathway was laid down when my first boyfriend at Camp Ramah in Utterson, Ontario, dumped me when he had to stand on a rock to kiss me and all the boys in his bunk made fun of him. The boys called me *tall girl* for the rest of the session. It may not have been the most creative taunt, but it bothered me and made me more self-conscious than I was already. Since my twelfth year, I have been attracted to tall men. I've tried a few times to put that aside because, as one man pointed out, we are all the same height lying down, but a preference is a preference, and this is mine. I have never cared about money, job title, or what kind of car a man drives, but the height thing is real.

On dating apps, you can set your preferences, and one of those is height. This is designed to keep people from wasting their time, and it is the one thing I appreciate about the whole process. It works well in a digital sense, but alas, it relies on the honesty and integrity of middle-aged Y chromosomes. A scholar friend of mine who wrote a fantastic book about the secret life of one of the most influential Jewish colonial families summed this up beautifully when she wrote simply:

And men lie. When it comes to deeply personal and intimate details, the lies often grow to the point where the liar and those adjacent begin to believe the lie.

Though I had vowed to take a break, it was days from April, and I decided to open the app late at night when I couldn't sleep. I found Rick, who'd sent me a very nice message a few days prior. A gallery owner in both Miami and the Hamptons of "modern art," his lineage was Puerto Rican and Cuban and he spoke several languages. All the boxes were ticked, and I noticed that he was also six feet one inch tall. I decided to come out of the dating retirement I never went into and go out with Rick. I sent him a cute message:

Thanks for the like. What's your favorite gallery in New York, and what language will you speak on our date?

We started a sweet little back-and-forth.

JOE TEXTED THE NEXT MORNING that he was sick and would be home for the rest of the week. For Joe to stay home sick from his job meant he was at death's door. He was the first man I'd ever known whose work ethic was more insane than mine, and I once went to work for a solid month with walking pneumonia. By coincidence, I'd made a huge pot of chicken soup that morning, which I usually make on Fridays but made on Tuesday because it was unseasonably cold. He pointed out that there were no accidents, and I felt bad for him. This is partly because I knew how sick he must have been to both stay home from work and tell me he was sick. I would be passing right by his exit as I drove out to meet Rick, so I told him that I would drop off a container of soup for him that afternoon late in the day.

My Year of Really Bad Dates

He wasn't kidding about how sick he was. When I arrived, he looked like hell. As a ginger, he was pale after a day in the sun, but now he looked pasty and literally couldn't get off the couch. Joe is a man who prided himself on taking care of everyone else and getting things done, this state made him miserable, and he looked it. I could relate as I am a terrible patient as well who hates being sick more than anything. Since I had been sick each month for the last six, my compassion was elevated even though I was angry with him. I still had a glimmer of hope that he would change his mind, though I wasn't sure why. Any normal person would have kicked his indecisive butt until hell wouldn't have it again, but I was clearly not in a normal headspace.

I looked fantastic, which he pointed out a minute after I arrived. I heated the soup in a pot on his stove while he lay on the couch across the room. He barely had the strength to move until I brought him the soup, and he attacked the bowl hungrily, slurping it down and asking for more. Watching him eat it made me laugh and I told him he might need a woman more than any man I'd ever met in my life, and he laughed. Then he looked at me lovingly and told me that I always made him laugh and that he missed that a lot. I took the opportunity to remind him that his blond real estate agent would never be able to make soup the way I could, nor do most of the things that I can do, and he agreed. I put the remaining soup in his fridge and told him to heat and eat the rest later that night and in the morning. He told me he loved me and thanked me profusely as I left to go on a date, which I was sure to let him know about.

Being in his half-packed-up condo broke my heart. All his things were about to be moved across the country into another woman's house, not mine. I wondered if he was going to take the antique compass I'd bought him. Would he squirrel it into a drawer away from Blondie, or would he put it out on his dresser, where it always laid open so he could see it and recall the time I brought it to him? I bought it at a small antique store in Charleston because he loved those kinds of things and because he had a compass tattoo on his arm.

The look on his face told me he was jealous, which I found interesting since he was planning to move to Phoenix and live with another woman. He told me several times yet again that it wasn't her but rather his family that he felt he needed to be closer to, but it still upset me to think about her. I didn't want to leave the apartment even though he was sick. I wanted to crawl onto the couch next to him and hold him and watch one of those stupid car shows he liked, throwing out snarky comments that made him laugh. Instead, I told him I thought he was an idiot and I headed out to the Hamptons for my date.

The Hamptons are located at the eastern tip of Long Island, otherwise known as the South Fork. It's a quilt of tiny towns that rims the ocean and is best known as a summer destination for the most affluent New Yorkers. It's filled with a strange mix of townies who live there year-round and psychotically wealthy New Yorkers who hide in their mansions behind enormous gates meant to keep out the riffraff. It is the birthplace of silly things like White Parties, where lily-white rich people wear white and show off their white privilege to one another, masking their white insecurities with their belief in their innate white superiority. The only people of color for decades were the bartenders and servers, who carried around the trays of hors d'oeuvres. God bless Andy Cohen and his *Real Housewives* franchise that brought the foolishness of the place to all of America, but I am not a fan of the Hamptons. In season, which is roughly Memorial Day to Labor Day, the traffic to get there is insanity because there is one road in and one road out of the area. Its elitism was always annoying, but with the advent and permeation of social media and reality television, the Hamptons have taken on a life of their own, raising the word *obnoxious* to dizzying new heights.

The Hamptons are quite a drive from my house, well over an hour, but Rick seemed interesting. We'd had a couple of nice conversations on the phone, though his voice seemed stilted, like he was putting on a voice rather than speaking to me in a voice. Because the winter had been so weirdly warm, the allergies and colds had been rampant, so I chalked it up to the idea that he was battling a cold. I was looking forward to seeing his art gallery too. He picked what he called an eclectic restaurant near his gallery on the quaint main street, and I pulled into the parking lot where he instructed me to go, though I was about fifteen minutes early.

I cautiously entered the restaurant looking around for him when the hostess, who introduced herself as Misty, approached to ask if she could help me. When I told her my name and that the reservation was for Rick, her smile vanished.

"Is this a date?" she asked. I was put off by the question. It seemed intrusive and I was self-conscious.

"Um, yes. A first date," I answered nervously.

"So, you haven't seen him before, have you?"

I started sweating. "I have not." *Where is Misty going with this?*

Misty explained that he'd selected a special table for me and led me toward the center of the restaurant. To be clear, the place was small, with maybe a dozen tables in the main dining room, and the table my date insisted upon was smack in the middle of the joint, and was the only one where the table was set side by side. This was not a seating arrangement I would choose, even if I liked the person. It's not easy to eat and carry on a conversation when you have to turn your head forty-five degrees throughout. Plus, I felt it wasn't the most comfortable way to get to know someone. My feet felt heavy as I walked to the table, but before I sat down, Misty had one more tidbit of information to share.

Short People Got No Reason

"Incidentally, Rick is about my height," she said.

Misty was wearing heels and only came up to my boobs.

It was too late to do anything other than batten down the hatches and hope at least he was a good conversationalist because in strolled my knight in shining armor. Rick glad-handed around the entire restaurant, speaking to every busboy, waitress, and bartender and most of the patrons before he finally made his way over to me. The vaguely confused and embarrassed looks on their faces indicated that most people either didn't know him or couldn't quite place who he was and didn't care. He was wearing an outfit that looked like he had just come from a Truman Capote dress-alike contest, complete with a Panama hat. It was early spring, and still cold outside, yet he was in a linen suit. I stood up to greet him, though it was clear that he was five feet five inches tall. I wondered how he came to write that he was six feet one inch tall on his dating profile. I did some quick dating math to try to figure it out as he sat down next to me. Math was never my thing, so this was the only equation I could come up with:

$$6'1" - 5'5" = 7"$$

Seven inches is the size of two credit cards, an iPad mini, or a #2 pencil.

At best, I imagined him filling out his profile, picking up those items, and thinking: *Gee, these things don't look very big. No woman will notice.*

Self-improvement is something I always strive for, so I told myself that he was smart and could carry on an interesting conversation based on our phone calls. That evening, despite his deception and the unusual table setting, wouldn't be a waste of time, and as a bonus, I hoped I would get the opportunity to see some interesting art.

As they say, hope springs eternal.

My Year of Really Bad Dates

As it turned out, I couldn't tell if he was a great conversationalist because he did all the talking. It was kind of like being at a one-man show that consisted of a ninety-minute monologue, with me as the only audience member. He told me all about himself, his life, and his background. He let me know that he was kind of a big deal in town and that the chef was a dear friend of his and would be sending out a lot of special food to delight us.

There are several schools of thought that women have about eating on dates. Some women are of the mind that eating light or picking conveys the image of daintiness, and that a real lady eats watercress and drinks mineral water. I subscribe to the opposite theory. I am a Jewish woman, raised and bred to eat. My mother made a three-course meal every night that consisted of a protein, a starch, and a vegetable (I especially loved canned spinach with a lot of butter). When I visited my grandparents in Brooklyn, my grandmother would call me the week before so I could order the menu of her cooking in advance, making sure to include all my favorites. Then, I would pass the phone to my father, who placed his order not only for what we'd eat there ("Yeah, the stuffed cabbage *with* the raisins, Ma") but also for takeaway that he planned to bring home to his buddies ("You know that Ron loves your coleslaw, better make it four pints"). When I was a child, each mother in my tight-knit neighborhood had her unique delicacies that would be brought to first communions, holidays, barbeques, and potlucks throughout the year. I have always felt that honesty in dating is the best policy. They may as well know in advance that this Jewess is an eater.

Rick ordered my drink for me, a fruity monstrosity that I would never drink let alone order. He then proceeded to order the meal for us, including a shrimp dish. I quietly mentioned to him that I was allergic to shrimp, which sent him into a tizzy.

"Are you sure? It's the best thing on the menu. You'll love it."

Short People Got No Reason

I assured him that I was positive about my allergies and that I didn't have an EpiPen, so he was welcome to eat the shrimp dish, but I would not partake since breathing was important to me. He didn't laugh at the joke but rather looked at me with pity, shrugged his shoulders, and told me I didn't know what I was missing. I felt like my life had been complete without shrimp. Besides, I was not in control of which foods I was allergic to, which amounted to only one. I decided not to continue the line of conversation, which was fine because the waitress started to bring dishes to the table. The food, a series of small plates and appetizers, came in a steady stream. I picked at it since most of the food was not what I would order. I was hungry when I pulled in, but I seemed to have a sudden lack of appetite. Though I was never a remotely picky eater, Rick somehow managed to order dishes that contained the three or four things I either didn't eat or didn't like. The chef never sent out anything, which didn't surprise me at all since I'm convinced he had no idea who Rick was, but the lack of free food blew Rick's mind. He spent a lot of the sixty-minute dinner wondering aloud why he did not receive the chef's bounty and even more time expounding on his greatness, his ingenuity, and his talent. Now and then, I glanced toward the door longingly as Misty and her coworkers winked and gave me looks that conveyed both sympathy and encouragement.

The meal was over, and he paid the check. I offered to help even though I'd only consumed about seven calories, but he insisted. My offer to go Dutch was the first full sentence I uttered for the entire meal, but no matter. Our dinner came to its conclusion, and I was almost lightheaded with joy that I was home free and could enjoy the long ride back, blasting the radio. Singing along to *'80s on 8* would be just the cure for the last hour. As we walked out the door, he invited me to check out his gallery, three doors down. I started to decline, but he explained that I

My Year of Really Bad Dates

had to go right by it anyway. The lot he'd instructed me to park in was directly behind his gallery and I didn't even notice it when I pulled in. I sighed, but at least I'd be able to see some cool art.

Wrong again. I'm always wrong. The shoe drizzle that had started outside began to smell like a full-blown shoe storm about to fall on my head. I braced myself as he unlocked the door, and I peered inside.

His gallery turned out to be one of those showplaces that have four (hideous) statues and two blown-up photographs. I always wondered how these places stayed in business and have been convinced that several in different cities I have seen are fronts for money laundering. There was one on Abbot Kinney Boulevard in Venice, California, where my ex-husband and I lived for a decade. The same pieces of etched glass stayed in the window for the thirteen years we lived in Los Angeles.

Unsurprisingly, the photographs were Rick's work. He wasn't a bad photographer. The composition was beautiful, and he captured the beach sunset well, though he was no Avedon or Arbus. I used the bathroom because it was a long ride home, and while I was in Rick's gallery restroom, one of my best friends texted to ask me if I wanted to watch our show. We've known one another since I was thirteen and he was sixteen, and we often joke that we share a brain. We were both late to the phenomenon of *The Walking Dead*, so now we watched it together, he in his city in Pennsylvania, me in New York. We text *Ready Set Play* and hit our remotes at the same time while we text one another snarky comments or jokes or *Ewwwwwww* when someone on the show dies a particularly gruesome death. I quickly texted him the *Reader's Digest* version of my evening, and he asked if I needed him to call me in ten minutes with an emergency, to which I exuberantly texted back, *Yes!*

Now that my escape would be clean and guaranteed, I left the bathroom with renewed energy to look at his other photograph

Short People Got No Reason

on the opposite wall, clutching my phone in my hand. Rick began a lengthy exegesis on the photographer's process and how he was pioneering the art form. I'm no photographer, but I am good friends with a famous one whose remarkable work marries social justice and art, and one of my best friends is a photo curator who has worked on shows in museums all over the world. As he expounded, his voice reminded me of something familiar. It was much higher than men's voices usually are but also had a nasal quality to it that sounded like a voice I knew well but couldn't quite place. He hadn't sounded like that on the phone, but the meal was so distracting that I couldn't focus on the tenor of my dinner partner's speech until we were standing alone in his echoing gallery. I was racking my brain trying to figure it out when I realized that ten minutes had come and gone. As I waited, the phone still in my hand, I willed my buddy to call, but he didn't. I made a mental note to murder him the next time I saw him. Another few minutes went by, and finally I told Rick I had a long drive home and had to leave immediately. That was the second full sentence I'd uttered all evening. He walked me to my car and tried to make out with me, but I told him I didn't think we were a good match, wished him well, and got in the car, trying not to peel rubber as I sped out of my parking space. As I drove away, the *'80s on 8* radio station played a commercial from a cartoon show I watched far too much of in my misspent youth. And then it hit me.

I had just spent ninety minutes with the Puerto Rican/Cuban version of Brainy Smurf.

This was the moment my buddy called, apologizing profusely for missing our ten-minute deadline. He is a baseball writer, and some early season trade was brewing so he lost track of time. I groaned and described my date, as well as my revelation about Brainy Smurf, and he laughed and laughed and let me know he would never let me forget this evening for as long as

My Year of Really Bad Dates

he lived. I let him know that wouldn't be much longer because I planned on strangling him the next time I saw him, but it didn't deter him from laughing both at me and with me. He suggested that maybe I take a break, and of course, he was right. He must have sensed a sadness in my voice because he stopped laughing and told me that I was wonderful and I would eventually find someone normal and worthy to spend time with. He is one of my best friends. He knows me better than most people and loves me dearly, and I know he wants the best for me, but even he didn't sound convincing that night.

I WALKED INTO CHAOS as usual when I got home. The house was a disaster, and my daughter was hysterically crying. She'd convinced herself that no college on planet Earth would accept her and that she had no talent. By the time I'd talked her off the ledge and threatened my son under penalty of his phone being taken if he didn't clear a path on his bedroom floor, it was late, and I was spent. As I fell asleep, Joe texted. He'd finished off my soup and he told me he was keeping the container in his fridge because every time he opened it, he thought of me.

I could have pointed out that, rather than being reminded of me by a plastic container in a cold box, he could have just come back to me and then he could see me whenever he wanted. I started to text that sentiment, but I stopped mid-thumb. What good would it have done to tell him to do that other than make me feel like his security blankie when he wasn't feeling well? I bet his new girlfriend probably couldn't talk to him or offer him comfort in his hour of need because she was likely showing a median-priced home in a Phoenix suburb to another blond that was likely screwing up someone else's life plan. I hearted the message and passed out, the theme song to *Smurfs* ringing in my ears.

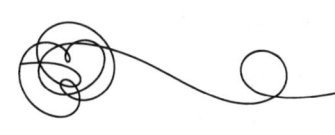

Dumb and Dumber

FOR THE FIRST PART OF MY LIFE, I was convinced that I was the world's biggest dolt. My parents were always telling me I acted dopey. To be fair, I did do a lot of dopey things as a kid, but then again, what kid doesn't?

For the formative years of my school life, I went to a religious Jewish day school where half of our days were spent on Hebrew language and religious instruction and the other half filled with the three R's in English. It was considered progressive because it was Zionist, because boys and girls shared a classroom, and because we learned Hebrew from actual native speakers of the language as opposed to the Yiddishized version of Hebrew. The school was ruled with an iron fist by a rabbi and his wife, both over six feet tall, with a shared interest in their disgust for most children, particularly me. I asked a lot of questions and talked all the time, which annoyed almost all my teachers and especially got under the skin of the principal, who was convinced educating girls past high school was a waste of time. My father hated the school and was constantly advocating for me to attend what he referred to as a "normal school."

He got his wish when times got tighter and the school raised tuition to rates my mother could not afford. I then attended public school, but the same issues persisted. I talked too much, I asked too many questions, and I had an aversion to homework, which

My Year of Really Bad Dates

I saw as busywork. I spent the four years of high school doing no homework and never studying for a test and still managed to finish in the middle of the pack. I certainly never distinguished myself as studious or academically inclined, and every report card brought a fresh volley of withering disappointment, eye rolls, and comments about spotty work. I was bored to tears with the construct of rote-memorization learning, which was essentially the concept behind the system in my small high school with teachers who should have retired years sooner. The median age of my instructors was about sixty-eight. The teachers talked at us, we took notes that we memorized, and then we took tests. I was always asking *why* questions, which got me into trouble yet again, so by senior year, I stopped speaking in class altogether.

When, in my AP English class, I was instructed to write a persuasive essay, I wrote about America's "New Best Friend" policy regarding Iraq and Iran. I pointed out that our troops were being shot at with the guns we had given Saddam to fight the religious zealotry of his neighboring country and that the war was foolish. The teacher was not only deeply Christian but incredibly conservative with a son in the Marines. She made every kid in her class say the pledge and told us that not supporting the war was tantamount to treason. She failed me and wrote on my paper, "Thank goodness nothing that you wrote in this essay is true!" She then proceeded to pull me aside after class to suggest that college was likely not for me and that I should consider beauty school. My mother was furious that I got an F.

By some miracle, I got into Boston University, and it was only there that I discovered that I might not be as stupid as everyone, including me, had always thought. I was taking a huge general history class with hundreds of kids, and after an essay exam was returned to me midway through the semester, the professor wrote a note on my blue book asking me to attend his office hours that

Dumb and Dumber

week. It was a postwar world history class, part of the required freshman course load. I tried to think of what I had done wrong, but nothing stood out. I barely had time for mischief anyway since I had to work close to full-time because I had no money to pay for food, transportation, or those all-important books that a freshman in college needed to attend classes. The class was going well for me, I was pulling an A, but as I leafed through the exam, I realized exactly why he wanted to see me. The essay question for the exam was part history and part interpretation of that history from a personal lens. So I decided to weave in a personal story about my family's postwar experience, written in flashback. I thought it would be interesting and creative, but clearly, I overstepped, and the professor, forced to read my drivel, wanted none of my experiment.

When I arrived at his office and sat down nervously, I had a whole apology speech prepared, including an offer to take the exam again. To my surprise, he seemed genuinely pleased to see me and shocked the hell out of me when he told me that reading my exam, passed to him by his TA, was the highlight of his week. He told me that I had a real affinity for both history and writing. This was the first time in my life that anyone had ever told me I had a talent for anything, and I was embarrassed by the praise. He asked me if I had declared a major, which I had not. He suggested history or international relations. He also suggested I go to the writing center to keep working on what he referred to as my "craft." My head was spinning after the meeting, and I went on to declare a double major in both history and international relations. When I graduated with honors, my parents were stunned. My father jokingly suggested that a calculation error had been made in the bursar's office.

I have always been attracted to intelligent men as friends and lovers. My ex-husband is a brilliant actor and talented writer with a degree from Harvard who can draw, sing, and play multiple instruments. The men I have been involved with for any extended period have been exceedingly bright in all kinds of ways, whether they were academic, mechanical, self-made, street smart, musical, or otherwise talented. In modern dating vernacular, this kind of attraction has been fetishized and is referred to as *sapiosexual*. I dislike this term, but it is now standard on dating apps when you list your preferences.

If you have never had the pleasure of using dating apps, allow me to share with you the myriad of new vocabulary words and acronyms that become your reality once you hit the Open button on your app screen. Thank goodness for Rabbi Google, since I was not well versed in such terminology before I began this journey, uphill in a blizzard twelve miles both ways to school. *Sapiosexual* is the easiest from the new lexicon. I'm no Latinist, but at least there are common roots that I can eke out on my own. The others, both abbreviations and fully spelled-out words, were like learning Hungarian. I finally put a reference list together on my phone, but here are some of the more indecipherable gems.

GGG: Good, Giving, and Game. With all due respect to Dan Savage, the writer who coined this turn of phrase, does anyone going into a relationship claim *not* to be good, giving, or game? Is there any dater out there who wants to declare themself Selfish, Stupid, and Stagnant? It's like when the Republican Party started talking about "family values" in the eighties and nineties. Are there any Democrats, nay, *any* politicians or political parties outside of the American Nazi Party, that publicly decry the family and any values that are supposed to go along with a family? It seems redundant to me, but you cannot find a dating profile today that doesn't proudly announce this intention.

DTF: Down to Fuck. I learned the meaning of this the hard way when, after exchanging fewer than six messages back and

Dumb and Dumber

forth with a man (and I use the term loosely, as he was more piglike than manlike), he asked me if I was DTF. In response, I naively texted: *It depends. What does that mean?* I received a laughing emoji as a response, so I turned to the Google machine. Call me old-fashioned, but if you want to ask a perfect stranger you have exchanged monosyllabic small talk with for two minutes to fuck you, it should be done in a full and grammatically correct sentence. I could at least respect the request if it had been done properly.

RIZ: short for *charisma* or *charismatic*. For some reason, fifty-year-old men now have decided to use middle school girl slang to describe their personalities. How about just writing, "I'm charismatic"?

Breadcrumbing: This term refers to someone who gives you enough attention to keep you interested, followed by periods of silence where they keep you away. I have seen this used as a warning label, and I fall for it whenever it comes to men, as in *No Breadcrumbing, Swipe Left*. If I were to use it in a sentence, it would go something like this: *Instead of making a decision based on emotions or integrity, Joe chose to breadcrumb Rachel for six solid months in the hopes that she would exclude herself from his life so he wouldn't have to take responsibility.*

Okay, that might be harsh, but I think I'm entitled to a little bit of bitterness. But on to my next VBD (Very Bad Date).

I never thought intellect would be an issue in online dating, but how foolish I was to hold on to this belief. Of the middle-aged men I have seen on dating apps, intelligence is rarely listed in their preferences when seeking a partner, and if it is, it is rarely listed as a priority or deal-breaker. My attraction to smart men only seems to limit my dating pool, since I must have an intellectual connection to someone to achieve a physical one. In the adventure that is online dating, I have met some very bright men, but in my experience, where they went to college or what they do for a living is not an indicator of their mental capacity or intelligence. I know Yale graduates who can't figure out how to buy a pack of construction paper at a drugstore.

I met Joshua for a drink. He lived two towns over from my little barrier island on the south shore of Long Island. He was an attorney and graduated from Columbia and Columbia Law. We decided to meet for a drink one evening even though we hadn't spoken on the phone first, which is not my MO. I made an exception because it felt less datey and more vibe-checky. Besides, it was a long dreary week in March, and I wanted a drink made by one of my favorite bartenders in town. Spring was right around the corner and the bar had two things I loved: a fireplace and small-batch Hudson Baby Bourbon, which is the perfect bourbon for an old-fashioned.

I arrived a few minutes early only to discover there were no seats available at the bar. It appeared that they had a rush minutes before I arrived, as people were just beginning to sip their drinks and some were in the process of ordering. There wasn't anywhere to wait, so I decided to get a table in the restaurant because I knew the place and they wouldn't care if a highboy for two only ordered drinks and an appetizer, and I was feeling a little peckish. They make amazing charred brussels sprouts with a balsamic glaze that I dream about, and just thinking about it made me drool. I ordered my drink and my food and told the waitress I was waiting for a first date to arrive.

Joshua walked in fifteen minutes late and found me at the table sipping my cocktail. He looked unhappy as he sat down, frowning.

"I see you sat at a table. I thought we were meeting at the bar. I don't do food on a first date because I date so much and spend so much money that I only do food if I think she's worth it."

Dumb and Dumber

I wasn't sure how to respond to that opening line, which I found deeply insulting. He'd known me for thirty seconds and had already decided I was not worth it, whatever that meant. I explained that there were no seats at the bar and that the wait would have been substantial, but he still looked skeptical when he took his seat across from me, as if my goal for the evening was to trick him into buying me a reasonably priced appetizer. The waitress came to ask him what he wanted, and he ordered a seltzer, plain. When she walked away, he looked me up and down, as though he were examining a painting.

"You look nothing like your photos."

His statement surprised me. Every other man I have ever met online has told me I looked exactly like my photos and has complimented me on my honesty. In truth, if I weren't such a Luddite, I'm sure I'd filter them like everyone else, but alas, I can barely figure out how to change my outgoing message on my voicemail. I'm no supermodel, but I do the best I can with what the Good Lord gave me, and since I've never broken a mirror when looking into one, I'm pleased with the way I look. Once again, I was speechless (I'm rarely speechless), but before I could process the train wreck of manners I had just experienced, he had already moved on to another topic by asking me how often I dated and what I was looking for in a mate. It came across as very clinical, almost like an intake interview, and it was clear that he was as appalled by me as I was by him. For a brief second, I considered bolting, but my dish arrived, and leaving two-thirds of a perfectly good old-fashioned should be considered a criminal act. Besides, I was fascinated by Joshua's oblivious nature about how he came across as a huge horse's ass to a total stranger.

As I munched, he told me that this was the fifth date he'd gone on this week. Seeing as it was only Thursday, I asked him when he had time to practice law, and he looked at me like I had

My Year of Really Bad Dates

three heads and eight eyes and explained to me like I was a three-year-old that what he referred to as "professionals" only date at night after a hard day's work. I loved that he thought I was not a professional. Also, there are all kinds of professionals, from boring lawyers that are at best moderately attractive to bus drivers. It was clear that he thought anyone without an Ivy League degree was beneath him, though if I were a betting woman, I would have wagered that both my CV and social circle were much more impressive than he could ever dream. But something new was gleaned from his statement, which was that I could cross humor off his list of attributes, along with tact, grace, and generosity. I started to wonder how repulsive Joshua could be, but I learned the depth to which he could sink quickly when he described the date he went on the night before.

According to him, it was going swimmingly. Unlike me, this woman was apparently worth a meal because he name-dropped a very expensive (and very mediocre) Italian restaurant on the Upper West Side that mostly caters to tourists, where he took her to dinner for their first date. He told me she looked even better than her photos, unlike his assessment of me, I supposed, and hung on his every word. This indicated to me that either she was a hooker or she didn't get out much. After he paid the check, he told me she invited him back to her place for coffee and dessert. When he got to this part of the story, he winked and said, "You know what it means when a woman invites you for 'coffee,' right?"

I sighed. I knew what he thought it meant. This woman could have simply been inviting him back to her apartment for an actual cup of coffee because she liked him, though I'd only spent fifteen minutes with the man, and that seemed unlikely to me, but who knew? Even a filthy, banged-up, stinky pot could have a lid that fit. I was curious to hear the story's finish, the end of which I could have predicted. He went back to her apartment

Dumb and Dumber

for coffee (using air quotes around *coffee* for the second time—I hate air quotes), and once he was on the sofa in her living room, the woman excused herself for a minute. When she returned, she was clad in a lace teddy and demanded $300 from him to continue. He feebly protested, but then she threatened to call her pimp, who she claimed was in a waiting car downstairs if he refused to pay. After some negotiation, they settled on $200, and he left the apartment.

I had been on the date for thirty minutes by this point. I thought it was clear to us both that we were not a match and would never see one another again, but I had to wonder why he shared that information with me. In the first place, it was not an impressive story, and he came off looking like the world's biggest idiot. In the second place, he paid for sex that he didn't have, which made him look like not only an idiot but also a complete eunuch. I couldn't help myself, so I asked him why he didn't just fuck her. He obviously found her attractive, she was a professional after all, and more importantly, he paid.

Again, he looked at me as though I had a pound of spinach in my teeth. He shook his head at me and said simply, "A guy like me doesn't pay for it."

I stifled my instinct to laugh, as it struck me that he was exactly the kind of guy who pays for it.

For a brief moment, I had a fantasy about telling him that, but in the end, I said nothing. What good would it have done? At some point, I knew he would meet some woman, and they would live in mediocrity ever after, while I would die alone, surrounded by cats that wanted to scratch my eyes out.

I suddenly lost my appetite halfway through my brussels sprouts, but my need to drink heavily was rising with each passing second. Once his fairy tale was complete and he finished the water he ordered, Joshua looked around the room, bored. He

My Year of Really Bad Dates

stood up, signifying that he was finished with the date and with me. I couldn't bring myself to either stand up or shake his hand, since he wasn't worth the energy it would have required, but I managed a small nod as he left the restaurant. I stared down at my half-finished drink and looked at my phone. I'd sat down at seven o'clock, Eastern Standard Time, and it was seven forty-two. I did some quick dating math. The date lasted forty-two minutes, minus the fifteen minutes that I spent waiting for him, but it felt like it lasted six hours. I decided to give the date the benefit of a full hour, so when I subtracted one from six, I concluded that despite the real time, the date was five hours long, which made it four hours and fifty-nine and a half minutes longer than it should have been.

I looked up to signal to the waitress, but she and her colleague were already looking at me and talking. She came to the table, ripped up the check, and directed me to the bar where the bartender had a fresh bourbon and a sympathetic smile. The crowd had cleared, and my server had heard a good chunk of the conversation but told me she knew, the second he walked into the place, she made him for a douchebag of epic proportion (her words, not mine, but spot-on). They told me I was a beautiful and very cool woman and that I should never go on a date with a man like that again. I was so overwhelmed by their kindness and understanding of my misery that I teared up.

AS THE MONTHS DRAGGED ON, I was starting to feel everything. Sometimes it felt like my grip on the day-to-day was so tenuous that it was hanging on by one frayed piece of dental floss. The strangest things made me cry or sent me into a shame spiral: a song I didn't like, or a photograph. Once, out of the blue, my ex-husband asked me how I was doing in a rare moment

Dumb and Dumber

of connection, and I started bawling. Anything that provided a thought or a hint of a whiff of any mistake I'd ever made sent me down a rabbit hole from which I couldn't return. The spinouts were starting to last longer by the week. When they'd started in the fall just before the World Series, they would take a few minutes. By the spring with the Knicks having an actual shot at the title, it sometimes took days for me to recover.

I was holding it together, even traveling for work or making dinner and doing all the things that I was supposed to do, but sleeping had stopped, and eating wasn't going well either. I needed something to change but wasn't sure what. It never occurred to me that something might have been professional help, or that the dark place I was in was much darker than even I understood it to be. I didn't know how to ask for help or what kind of help I even needed. I was not supposed to need help; I was always the one who provided the help. I had a feeling that it was me. That I was broken and if I just worked harder on moving forward, everything would go back to normal, but now I wasn't sure what normal was, or even if I wanted things to go back to how they were. My default mode was always to work harder, but that didn't seem to help anymore. Though I couldn't admit it to myself, the truth was that working harder never worked.

My daughter starred in her school musical that spring, as she had every year since she was a sophomore in high school. She was the villain Ursula in *The Little Mermaid*, and it was a great part for my future character actor child. The show was set to open in a few days, and it had been a rough week for all of us. She rehearsed late into the night, still had not heard about college admissions, and was exhausted physically and emotionally. Rather than be excited for the last performance of her high school career with her besties at her side, she spent every night that week crying herself to sleep. Her grandfather (whom she idolizes) would not be in attendance. This wasn't shocking. He rarely showed up in our lives, and he rarely spent more than twelve to twenty-four hours a year with my kids. Part of this was his exhaustive work schedule, but the other part, more significant to our story, was that his relationship with his son is a difficult one, and since he never liked me and is a conflict-averse man, he mostly pretended we didn't exist. I know he adores my children, but because the relationship with their parents was always at best strained and we were never invited, my kids have never spent a holiday with their paternal extended family. They've never blown out birthday candles, eaten a turkey leg, or spent a family vacation with them either. They don't discuss it much, but it bothers them, and on rare occasions, they have cried over the situation. My ex-husband and I have come to peace with this, but the kids haven't quite gotten there yet.

His absence was not the main reason for the tears, however. My daughter cried daily because she was constantly reminded by all the adults surrounding her that she had no extended family to support her regularly. The costume lady, teachers, cafeteria workers, and people she bumped into on the street in our beach town with a year-round population of thirty thousand asked her when her famous grandfather was coming to see the show. When she would tell them he was not coming, they acted surprised and felt the need to ask her why. She didn't have the answer other than he was busy, but this wasn't enough. They expressed sadness and outrage that he would not see her perform.

I understood that people were fascinated by celebrities, but they didn't know or understand our specific family dynamic, and frankly, it was none of their business. I'd spent her whole life making excuses for why her dad's family never showed up. Mostly, I blamed myself, which is what I have always done in my life. When my children asked me why everyone in Dad's family

Dumb and Dumber

was spending a holiday together without us, I always told them I couldn't afford to take them, or that I had to work and we couldn't go. Then they would cry and tell me I was a mean mommy who worked too much. My ex-husband let me take that fall for years. I couldn't do it anymore. All I could do was comfort her, and after a particularly bad evening, I wrote a Facebook post asking people to leave her be, as I feebly tried to explain my feelings.

This was a huge leap for me. I never publicly share my feelings about anything, let alone about my ex-husband's family. In their rulebook, any hurt they inflict upon anyone at any time is to be taken like a well-trained dog enduring a child tugging at its tail, never barking or nipping. There is never an apology offered or an explanation given. The two or three times I pushed the issue in the twenty-five years I was with my ex-husband, they either told me I was a drama queen, said they had no idea what I was talking about, or simply screamed at me and told me I needed to lower my "expectations." It was a foolish thing to do, but I suppose in some way that silly Facebook post was some kind of cry for help—a lame, stupid, and ridiculous cry, but a cry nonetheless.

I was rewarded by being cut off by my ex-husband's few remaining family members who still spoke to me. I got a text message from his cousin, whom I considered a dear friend, saying that she hoped the members of her family wouldn't see the post as it would preclude them from having a relationship with my children.

It was interesting to me that not one member of this illustrious family paid an ounce of attention to me during the three miscarriages and the ectopic pregnancy that almost killed me. They stood as silent witnesses while I was humiliated time and again. Nobody lifted a finger to help when my ex-husband was debilitated by depression and utterly unhinged. Suddenly, one Facebook post, the first time I *ever* stood up to the nonsense in twenty-five years, was so terrible that it would preclude them from having a relationship with my children. Not that any of them had much of one at the time, but still. Their family motto should be "Every man for himself." They should embroider that on pillows and sell them.

No matter, I thought, drying my tears from a particularly long and vomit-inducing crying jag. I knew that soon I would be traveling to Israel with our children and one of my best friends from childhood. I had not been to Israel since the pandemic hit, and I missed it terribly. The last time I was there, mere days away from the global lockdown, was for my work as the vice president of one of Israel's largest museums. There was a movement afoot to reclaim the country from the grip of its right-wing ruling prime minister, and I wanted to see it for myself. I wanted to show my children that if people worked together, there was nothing they couldn't accomplish. As a bonus, there were few people with whom I could laugh as hard and as freely as my friend Celia. She knows me so well that we have a kind of shorthand between us that makes traveling with her easy and fun.

That's the ticket, I thought. Two weeks with Celia and the kids in the Holy Land would set me straight, and when I returned, everything would be better.

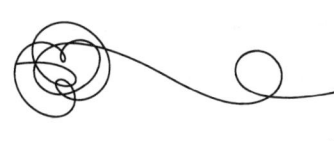

Girl Getaway

IT WAS THE LAST WEEK IN MARCH at six thirty in the morning, Eastern Standard Time, and I was driving to a dance competition trying to figure out where my life went so wrong. I was soon going to be traveling to my favorite country, but at that moment, I was preparing for a torturous day. My son, fifteen years old at the time, is a competitive dancer who is monstrously talented. When he isn't dancing four hours a day, five or six days a week, he is dancing in the basement or in my bedroom or twirling in the kitchen as he fixes his after-school snack. In the evening, as I wind down from the day, he often appears in my bedroom asking if he can show me something he's been working on. It's like a nightly floor show and he brings me unimaginable joy.

The dance competitions, however, bring only sorrow.

It was a novelty when my son first began attending these hideous events. I thought he would go to a few, twirl around with his friends, and we'd come home and forget all about it. That was over eleven years ago. Now, from March through May, we endure what is known to us unfortunate parents as "Competition Season." It is a difficult phenomenon to explain as the English language lacks both the vocabulary and case structure for any reader to fully grasp its true horror.

Picture it: Long Island, 2023. A beautiful middle-aged mother arrives at a high school auditorium. If it is hot outside,

My Year of Really Bad Dates

the air conditioning inevitably will not be turned on yet. If it is cold outside, the heater will invariably have been turned off. It is therefore advisable to dress in layers that you can peel or add to depending on the situation. Hundreds of girls ranging in age from five to eighteen are made up like two-dollar whores. Their hair is shellacked to within an inch of its life and plastered to their foreheads. Some are wearing costumes that would make a seasoned hooker who strolls the boulevard blush and that often includes feathers, thongs, and even pasties. Mothers are wearing T-shirts and sweatshirts with images of their daughters' faces splashed across their chests with the words "Kick-Ass Dance Mom" emblazoned on the front and back. The decibel level is so loud that my joints vibrate, and the music is mostly terrible, eclipsed only by the grating voice of the emcee wearing clothing decades too young for his or her age. If you put aside the cultural appropriation (think of suburban white children in what they believe to be hip-hop attire or wearing Asian pajamas from Chinatown and bowing to one another), the fake eyelashes, and the adults living vicariously through their children, there still isn't enough caffeine in the world to make spending eight hours at a dance competition bearable. For some reason, unfathomable to the average brain, studios choose these competitions to make social commentary on homelessness, war, child abuse, and violence through lyrical or contemporary leg lifts and splits. I await the day when I will hear, "Please welcome entry number 412 to the stage, 'The Jews Are in the Attic Up There,' a lyrical small-group number."

    Luckily, my son has been part of the same team for a decade, and the other mothers are very like-minded, which makes the untenable tolerable. We gossip, sit, laugh, sweat, shiver, and make Starbucks runs together. I bring donut holes from Dunkin'; they find my son's jazz shoes and drive him because they are more "fun" than I am. We are sisters in suffering and a few of them are now close friends.

I arrived at the venue, a community college in Suffolk County about forty-five minutes away, at seven fifteen in the morning. The knowledge that I would be there until after eight o'clock that evening depressed me. My son got situated in his dressing room. Now that he was a teen, he could pretty much take care of his own costume changes, hair, and shoes. All I needed to do was provide occasional zipper support and dollar bills to feed the machines for the candy and soda that kept him going. The downtime stretching before me seemed endless, so I started by looking for coffee, only to discover that there was none to be had. The coffee kiosk was not yet open, and leaving in search of coffee was not possible since I would miss the opening number, which my son specifically asked me to watch. My favorite dance mom and aunt, Regina and Meaghan, were not there yet, and I texted furiously demanding that they arrive immediately and bring copious amounts of Starbucks.

This was the moment when Joe texted to ask me how it was going. He was still here in New York, though his departure for Phoenix was quickly approaching. I wished he would leave just so I knew he was gone and out of my life, but I was also panicked about him going. Despite everything, I was so desperate for relief and support that I didn't want him to leave.

He wanted to know how it was going. I responded with the following text message:

I'm at a dance competition. There is no coffee. I wish I were dead.

He sent a laughing emoji, asked me where I was, and mercifully offered to bring me a coffee on his way home from the gym. He was leaving for his new life with his dopey blond in a week, and I realized it would likely be the last time I would see or communicate with him.

My Year of Really Bad Dates

He showed up with the coffee and I walked out to the parking lot where he was waiting in his car. I went with him to pick it up last spring, and he was so excited. It's an electric Mustang with a huge touch screen, the seventh Mustang he has owned and the first since he sold his tricked-out red Mustang when he got divorced four years earlier.

I got into the car, thanked him profusely, and slurped the coffee. On the car's screen was his blond real estate agent's name with a red heart. My name used to have the heart next to it, and I told him it was tacky, though I secretly wished the heart was next to my name again. He told me he was sad, and that he was tired of saying goodbye to people. He feared his new life but was plowing ahead. He asked me to kiss him goodbye and I did, but I couldn't help but feel that it wasn't what either of us wanted. He also let me know he would be leaving New York on April 1, which made me laugh hysterically.

"How fitting! The biggest fool I know leaving on April Fool's Day!" He laughed. I still made him laugh.

"Your Tupperware is still in my fridge, you know. I'm taking it with me."

"Why?"

"You know why. I love you, Rachel."

"You fucking moron."

I exited the vehicle and went back into the dance competition. I didn't turn around to watch him drive away.

I couldn't stop crying in an empty bathroom I found in a faraway corner of the theater. The crying jags were becoming problematic because as much as I wanted to, I no longer had any control over when they started or stopped. They came on hard and fast, and I couldn't make them stop until I had no more tears to cry, which took anywhere from ten minutes to two hours. This bout was relatively short, and after about fifteen sobbing minutes, it was over. I washed my face and returned to the simulacrum of hell that was taking place in the auditorium. I found Regina and Meghan and stuck to them like glue all day. Joe texted on and off, and even though I knew I shouldn't have responded, I did. He was sad about leaving.

I can't believe I'm really leaving New York for good.
Getting sick of saying goodbye to people all day every day. Oof.
I'm scared, but I think this is what my heart is telling me to do.

I tried to be a mixture of funny, empathic, and gentle, but I teared up with every text. I was leaving for Israel the day he was leaving for Phoenix.

It makes me sad that we won't travel and see the world together. I'd love to go to Israel with you.

He still had me on a hook, and I couldn't release myself from its hold. Nobody in his life knew that we were communicating or how he felt about me, and I realized he kept his life utterly compartmentalized, just like my ex-husband. I should talk. None of my friends wanted to hear me mention his name ever again, so nobody in my life knew the situation either. Hours went by, and I received this text from Joe:

Who knows what the future holds? Maybe I'll come back and marry you.

I stared at the text for a long time. Then I started to cry again. But it felt different. For the first time, it felt angry.

I had a fantasy that he would show up on my doorstep the day he was supposed to leave for the airport, like in the last episode of *Friends*, where Rachel didn't move to Paris after all so she could be with the love of her life. What if Joe was the love of my life? I didn't think that he was despite my childish dreams because the love of my life wouldn't leave me for a blond real estate agent. I was furious that he would dare to text me something like that. Also, Joe lives in his head. I wasn't sure how to respond to his text, so I didn't.

My Year of Really Bad Dates

Of course, I knew he wasn't coming back, and I knew he would be married to Blondie by the end of the year like I knew how to spell my name. Joe, by his admission, is a guy who cannot be alone, and she was his gift with the purchase of his new life, like the ugly shade of lipstick Lancôme gives you when you buy toner and moisturizer. He'd told me one hundred times that it wasn't a choice between me and that silly woman, but rather he was choosing between me and his family. I couldn't compete with his family, nor would I have wanted to, but the fact that we were still engaged in our weird dance crossed the line from strange to absurd that final day. I couldn't wait for him to leave in the misguided notion that once he was gone, I'd be fine, but I was also terrified of him leaving. I see now that our weird cha-cha was all that was holding me together. He was the boundary between the me I presented to the world and the darkest, saddest, angriest parts of myself that I could never deal with or had the time to explore. Now it seemed I wasn't just exploring them—I had discovered them all. The feelings were angry that I had disturbed them, like a native tribe that reacted in fury when the white "saviors" showed up to explain that they'd been doing everything all wrong. "Your Jungle God is lovely, but have you heard of Jesus Christ?"

I finally collapsed into bed at nine-thirty that night, just in time to get a phone call from my best friend and college roommate, Lynn, who lives around the corner from me. We were both turning fifty that year, but we couldn't come up with an idea for how we should celebrate. When she called me, she was precise and matter-of-fact as she explained that she'd purchased airline tickets for us to Miami for the weekend and we were going to celebrate together. She got the tickets, and it was up to me to find us a hotel room on the beach for the weekend. She meant business. I agreed without hesitation, even though I'd be leaving for Israel less than forty-eight hours after I returned. I didn't care.

Girl Getaway

We were going to celebrate come hell or high water, and there was no room for debate or discussion.

AFTER THREE MONTHS OF BEING COLD, a warm place where we spent a lot of time both during and after college was going to be nothing short of delightful. And it was. We got bikes and rode down South Beach, visiting all our old haunts along the way from the cafés to the salsa clubs. We reminisced about all the grouper sandwiches we consumed with my father, about the time we stole my evil stepmother's sports car and went clubbing, and about our late-night mani-pedis while we gossiped and laughed. We ate Cuban food, Italian food, and ice cream along with everything else the fabulous city has to offer. We drank out of coconuts on the white-sand beach. We even tried to stay up late, but we couldn't wear heels like we used to, and the music was loud in the lounge. Not to brag, but we were let in and brought to the front of the line, which we both counted as a victory.

On our last day, I got a message from Steve, or My Music Man, as he appears on my phone.

Steve is one of my favorite people. He is hilarious and creative, and we both went to Boston University, six years apart. We dated for almost a decade back when my marriage was open and through my divorce. We have taken breaks here and there—sometimes his marriage would close and sometimes life got in the way—but for the better part of ten years, we would meet every six or eight weeks, have dinner, drink bourbon, check into a hotel, and screw each other's brains out for hours. It may have been the most perfect relationship of my life. No big responsibilities, but plenty of laughs, great sex, and a lot of great vibes between us. I once joked that when our kids were up and out, I should move into the studio behind his house in Brooklyn and become a sister to his wife, whom I liked a lot. I suggested that she could have him 70 percent of the time, and I would take the remaining 30.

"Oh please," he'd responded. "She's already sick of me. By then, she'll want the 30 percent."

I loved the big palooka, but if I'm being honest, I was angry with him and had been for a few months. I'd reached out to him when Joe dumped me, and he was very sympathetic but also told me that he felt like he "couldn't give" me what I "needed" and that I was "looking for something permanent" that he could not provide. I had barely spoken to him since.

Steve read my last newsletter and liked it, so he texted to say that it had cheered him up immensely since he was in South Florida taking care of his dying mother who was once again hospitalized for congestive heart failure. (Of course, this fact never stopped her from smoking a pack a day, which drove him to the brink of madness.) I told Steve that I too was in South Florida, and he immediately wanted to get a hotel room in Miami for us as soon as visiting hours were over at the hospital. Lynn and I conferred, and she was cool with the scenario, but the more I thought of it, the less cool I was.

I hadn't seen him in months, and I was still annoyed with him. I understood the male midlife crisis, but this was not the first rodeo I had been to with My Music Man where he panicked and backed off. Every other year or so, he would decide, on my behalf, that he was holding me back and that we should no longer sleep together. Steve seemed to believe he was the reason I had not found my true love. I was pretty sure there were a few other reasons, like, oh, let's say a divorce that wrecked me, the crushing responsibility of being a single mother of two teens, lawsuits, death, and the destruction that had peppered my life for the last five years. Whenever he would flip on me, I always told him that it was his choice and I'd miss him, and he always came back within a week or a month.

Girl Getaway

But this last time felt different. I was exhausted from the men who made decisions for me and about me without bothering to ask me what I might have wanted and needed. My father controlled through aggression, and my ex-husband through passive aggression. As of the writing of this book, I am still not divorced because he refuses to move forward, respond to legal letters, or sign papers.

My in-laws never cared enough about either of us to control anything, but they did constantly make me feel like I was beneath their station and was the problem. If they didn't like something my husband did or said, it was attributed to my "doing," as though I was some puppeteer pulling the strings while twirling my penny-dreadful mustache.

My father was dead, and my mother always blamed me for everything negative that ever happened in my life. When I told her I got a job in Buffalo that would save us from losing our house, her immediate response was, "Well, you lucked out given that you never should have been there in the first place. You better not be making more money than I was making when I retired in Buffalo." When my ex-husband and I were separating, she asked me what I had done. She was always like this. Was it any wonder that I only seemed to be attracted to men who withheld, struggled with control issues, or were undecided about their life paths?

By the time evening descended, Steve texted that his mother was agitated and that he wasn't comfortable leaving her. I would have loved to get laid well, and Steve is magnificent in bed. The last great sex I'd had was with Joe seven months ago, and yet, rather than disappointment, I felt relief. Lynn and I had a great last night eating, giggling, and talking until we passed out.

Lynn left very early in the morning to fly to DC for a conference, and I had breakfast by the pool before my early afternoon flight, feeling very content. My phone gave off that familiar ding

My Year of Really Bad Dates

that told me another suitor was awaiting my answer. I opened the app to find a very sexy, adorable, completely fucked-up man, so of course I was attracted to him. He was six feet five inches, a writer, and an English teacher. Based on his witty opening to me (*Come here often? Now give me a better opener*), he was also funny and smart. The fact that he was fifty-one and had never been married was a bit of a red flag, but maybe he was worth a try. I would deal with him when I returned, since I had to get home and pack up the kids for Passover in Israel, a country I passionately loved, on the brink of civil war. Good times.

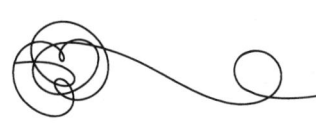

For the Love of All That Is Holy

THE KIDS AND I ARRIVED in Jerusalem after a long layover in Munich and a fourteen-hour flight. We met our friends at a hotel near the Old City. Celia had not been to Israel in more than twenty-five years, and her children and my son had never been. I'm the only one out of the six of us who speaks Hebrew, and we had an ambitious if not fluid itinerary. I was certain it was going to be a fun trip, and I thought it was just the thing I needed to snap out of the hell I was going through internally.

Being in Israel is complicated. I love being there, the people, the culture, the food, the language, and the history. The politics is another story, best saved for a later tome, but part of the reason I wanted to come was the political moment the country was experiencing. After a lifetime of progressive leftist Zionism, I wanted to see the citizens of the country I love take a stand for its original core values. For the first time, I saw Israeli citizens more unified than divided, which made me happy. I also saw and heard a sense of sadness and resignation that I was not used to hearing from my friends and former colleagues. Of course, I had no idea what was in store for us by October of that year.

It always surprises Israelis that I speak Hebrew fluently and am not Israeli. Typically, when I am traveling and I interact with

My Year of Really Bad Dates

Israelis, the conversations with cab drivers, waiters, and people I randomly bump into always go pretty much the same way:

"Why you speak Hebrew so good?"

"Oh, I don't know. I learned from native speakers."

"Your mother is Israeli?"

"No."

"Your father?"

"No."

"But you speak Hebrew like Israeli."

"Um, thanks."

"Where you living?"

"New York."

"Why you don't live here?"

We started in Jerusalem, where I acted as the buffer for Celia. Throughout our lives, we have played this role for one another. Once in New York, she came out for a drink with me and my father-in-law after seeing him in a play. I thought we were just having a casual drink with my father-in-law to make awkward small talk for an hour. However, when we arrived at the trendy actor bar, sans sign out front, his wife was lying in wait for me, drumming her fingers on the table with a sinister look on her face. My sister-in-law and her strange boyfriend were there as well. It was like a community theater version of *Intervention*, and I panicked. I had been set up for something, but I had no idea what I had done or why this was happening. Celia texted me under the table:

I'm not leaving you alone. This bitch is out for your blood.

She sat with us for as long as she could, but eventually, my mother-in-law looked her dead in the eye and said:

"You need to leave right now."

The minute she left, the claws came out. Or at least, the swearing like a sailor on shore leave coupled with her unending love for humiliating me came out.

For the Love of All That Is Holy

"You fucking asshole piece of shit! I'm sick of you and your bastard husband."

Her voice was loud and the acid jazz music in the bar played too softly to cover her rage. She spent hours berating me as I silently wept, knowing that any noise I made would be considered "dramatic." Famous actors, who had just arrived and couldn't exactly see what was happening in the dark corner of the bar, kept approaching the table to say hello to my father-in-law, and he would pretend that we were having a lovely family visit.

"Fred! Have you met my daughter-in-law?" he said to Alfred Molina as he looked confused and acknowledged me, the sobbing woman.

"Richard! I'm running to see your show as soon as mine closes! You remember my daughter-in-law, right?" Richard Thomas, whom my ex-husband adores, looked concerned as he scurried away at the first opportunity.

After two hours of being abused and humiliated, I excused myself to use the bathroom located on the opposite side of the bar. As I walked past the last table in the corner, I felt a hand tap my wrist. It was Liev Schreiber and his then wife Naomi Watts at a table with several of their friends. He said, "We don't know what's happening over there, but we're on your side."

When the celebrities are watching *you*, there is a significant problem.

I took the abuse for another hour, finally excusing myself to leave. I still had the delusional idea that fighting back or standing up for myself would make things worse. I learned this from my ex-husband, who spent years of his life enduring this kind of abuse, gaslighting, and cruelty. His stepmother had been in his life since he was eight and married his father by the time he was nine. His philosophy was always to just endure it until it was done and then not speak of it again. Every time he tried to call out the dysfunction, it made his situation worse. The unwritten family law was that everyone had to endure the torment while it was happening, and then we were all expected never to speak of it again, move on, and "get over it." Apologies were never issued. Rather, if they later decided that they may have overstepped a wee bit (I mean, what they consider overstepping would inspire the average bear to never speak to them again), his stepmother sent his father to us the following day with a loaf of zucchini bread, which was supposed to serve as the apology, though it was couched as "We thought you'd like this. You're welcome."

I threw out that zucchini bread in two states multiple times over twenty-five years.

As terrible as I felt, it was my ex-husband's situation that always broke my heart and still does when I think of what he endured from the time he was nine. When I got back to my friend's apartment where I was staying that night, I texted Celia, thanking her. She couldn't hold off the nightmare forever, but her presence stopped at least an hour of the ultimate insanity, and for that, I was grateful.

Celia's mother is an unmedicated manic depressive. Her older sister has a dozen children and lives in a settlement. Celia had not seen her in sixteen years. It was my turn to be her buffer, and I was more than happy to return the favor.

WE WALKED THROUGH THE OLD City, visited with Celia's sister's family, and had dinner in her mother's apartment. It wasn't nearly as bad as it could have been, and our kids love one another, which was icing on the cake. We ate huge trays of *knafe*, pastries, and shawarma and gorged on the greatest breakfasts in world history. If you have never had the pleasure of eating breakfast in

For the Love of All That Is Holy

Israel, you are missing out on one of the greatest culinary pleasures a person can savor.

Passover in Israel is always madness. I sensed a lot of tension in Jerusalem and wanted to get as far south as we could before the chaos erupted in full swing. Sure enough, the day we boarded the bus to get to the Dead Sea, Jerusalem plunged into its annual lunacy with dueling protests, Israelis getting totally out of hand in the Arab Quarter and shutting down Al-Aqsa.

We stayed at a fabulous resort for a few days, resting and relaxing, and then moved even farther south to Eilat, where we hung at the beach, went to the aquarium, and had a makeshift seder with grilled chicken and lamb sausages, and Celia and I laughed all night as we compared our really bad dates. She shared her nicely curated selection of the most absurd profiles that she'd received on her phone, which was impressive in both its sheer number and level of awful.

We ended our trip in Tel Aviv. It was a wonderful time, and I was exhausted. We stayed in my favorite little hotel that has the best breakfast in the city and hosts a free afternoon tea from four to six that has not only booze but an all-you-can-eat buffet of delicious finger foods. When I stay there for business, I never have to spend money on food because the breakfasts and teas are so plentiful, and though the rooms are the size of postage stamps, it is right across the street from the beach, and I love the location and the quiet.

On our last night, I took the kids to my favorite little café on Dizengoff, and the waitress and I struck up a conversation. She asked me when we were leaving, and I told her the following morning. Rather than encouraging me to stay longer or move there permanently, she simply said: "Good. Right on time. Get your kids out of here before things get worse." How prescient she was.

My Year of Really Bad Dates

The cab driver the next morning shared a similar sentiment when he encouraged me not to return until everything was "settled." I felt maudlin and uneasy on the flight home instead of reflecting on the magic of the trip and being back in one of my favorite countries again after a three-year hiatus. I thought for sure that the trip would cheer me. Instead, I felt much worse than I'd felt before I left. Joe left on April 1 and did not text me to say goodbye or tell me he was thinking of me. I would likely never see or hear from him again, and that thought filled me with unspeakable anxiety. It reminded me of when my childhood blanket caught fire on our space heater one evening, and I had to relearn how to sleep without her (yes, it was a girl). My dreams were filled with terrifying endless falls through space or drowning in the ocean. The Nazi dreams returned too. In Israel, they came roaring back.

The Nazi dreams have been present periodically for my entire life, but they intensify when I am experiencing stress or turmoil. When Trump was elected, they crept back in slowly. When my father died and I was going through my separation, the dreams became even more vivid. I can remember having them as early as kindergarten. My teacher, Mrs. Anna Post, was a Survivor, and I knew where Auschwitz was before I knew where Cleveland, two hours away, could be found on a map. My grandparents were all Polish and lost virtually their entire families in the Holocaust.

At twenty-two, I started what ultimately became my career at the Shoah Foundation, Steven Spielberg's nonprofit that he founded with the full proceeds of *Schindler's List*. I worked for the foundation full-time for five years, and in the end, our team interviewed over fifty-two thousand Survivors in more than fifty countries in thirty-eight languages. I worked on the history team, and part of my job was to check the quality of the interviews and provide feedback to the interviewers. In looking back at my journals and notebooks from that time, over five years I likely watched two to three thousand interviews in three languages. I heard the worst that humanity has to offer and the greatest stories of resilience and courage that have likely ever been told. I went on to be the CEO of the Los Angeles Museum of the Holocaust for seven years after graduate school. I owe the Shoah Foundation my professional life and learned more in five years there than I would have in three PhD programs.

Generational trauma is no joke, as evidenced by a lifelong fear I have of cars backfiring, German shepherds, and large groups of drunk men singing in bars. These things trigger me. Once, when one of my best friends, Maya, and I were traveling in Ireland, we stumbled into a Dublin bar in the middle of the World Cup and found a group of German tourists singing "Das Deutschlandlied" while raising their beer steins filled with Guinness. I almost fainted. Her grandparents were Survivors too, and we both fled like we were about to be selected for "resettlement in the East." When we got down into the street, panting from the effort of running down several flights of stairs, Maya looked at me and said, "I think we're good now."

I nodded but then added, "You know, we were still good in there, right? I mean, they are just kids watching a soccer game."

She nodded but very wisely added, "What can I say? Epigenetic trauma is our thing. Let's go get something to eat." We didn't discuss it again.

When my father died, I found what amounted to a grab 'n' go bag in his safe-deposit box. It was filled with pieces of gold, stamps, cash, and things that could be carried easily and used in case, as his friends told me in all seriousness, the Nazis came back.

My Nazi dreams are almost always the same. I am in hiding somewhere very quiet and dark when the door flies open, and I am grabbed by uniformed SS officers, who drag me away into the abyss kicking and screaming. In these dreams when I was a child, I was taken from one of my parents; later it was my husband. Now, the dreams star my children, calling out for me as they are ripped away and I am shot and tossed into a mass grave while I'm still alive. I've tried almost everything in my power to banish these nightmares, but nothing has ever worked long-term. I was starting to believe nothing would ever work.

ONE NIGHT AFTER WE RETURNED HOME from Israel, it occurred to me that when I was with Joe, I never had Nazi dreams. Maybe that had been his secret hold over me. Was he my security blanket? Why did Joe have the superpower to banish the dreams away? Or did he? When I was with him, my life was quiet and simple. It revolved around my children, him, and writing my novel. It was the calmest year I had ever experienced as an adult. Was Joe the catalyst, or was he in the right place at the right time? I wasn't sure, and by then, I wasn't sure it even mattered. I was hopeful the Nazi nightmares would just fade, as they did typically when things calmed down. I had no idea how intense things would soon become.

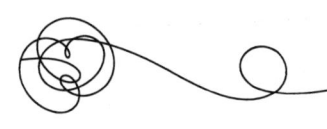

Dick Pics

DESPITE THE NAZIS COMING FOR ME in my dreams on a nightly basis, I started an adorable correspondence with Matt. He was the English teacher and writer who hit me up back in Miami, and he messaged me while I was away in Israel too. He was very funny, and I could tell that there was something edgy about him, which I needed in a date. We exchanged banter for weeks and I finally asked him if we were ever going to meet. He responded the next day by telling me he wasn't sure what he wanted, or even if he wanted to date. That confused me, since he was a paid member of a dating site, so I stopped initiating text messages, thinking that it was time to move on, but he then pursued me vigorously until I responded. We chatted on the phone, and as it turned out, he'd written a book on a subject that I found interesting. We exchanged essays and I liked the way he wrote. His talent impressed me. He seemed impressed by my work as well. He was dry and very funny both on the phone and over text, and he was beginning to tick my boxes.

We finally decided to meet, and he invited me over to his house to sit in his backyard and have a glass of wine. Now, I am aware that this is a foolish thing to do under any circumstance given that I did not know this man. But I made an exception because he wasn't too far away and he gave me his last name, where he worked, and the name of the paper in which he had a weekly column. I did a deep dive online and he was legitimately who he said he was, and he had no record. I gave two friends his address and told them I would check in with them when I arrived and via phone call when I left.

I dressed casually but adorably for the date in a form-fitting sweater and my favorite jeans and heels, which show off my best, ahem, assets. I wore high heels, higher than normal, because he was six feet five inches and we had talked about how it was difficult for him to talk to women sometimes because he had to hunch. When I showed up, he smiled and told me I looked even prettier in person than I did in my photos. His house was immaculate and charming, and he had set out a charcuterie tray for us to nibble on while sitting on his back patio, which was beautiful and perfectly landscaped. We had a fantastic evening and shared a delicious kiss that I knew in an instant would lead to sex. I don't sleep with people on a first date ever, but in his case, I made an exception, in part because I was lonely and in part because something about him felt right.

And yet, as it turned out, it was all wrong.

I didn't realize that he had consumed several drinks before I arrived, and while he held his liquor beautifully, his performance was much less . . . beautiful. He could not get it up, and he was embarrassed but laughed it off. The first time with someone new is often a throwaway. First, there is a getting-to-know-one-another factor that engenders inhibition. Second, there is a shyness in an oh-my-God-this-person-is-seeing-me-naked-for-the-first-time kind of way.

He seemed not to take it too seriously though, which was a great sign that he wasn't insecure or weird about sex. I felt good about the situation as I drove home. I wondered if this new distraction would get rid of the darkness for a while, or at least push it away so I wouldn't have to feel it anymore.

Dick Pics

The next morning, he texted early to say hello and let me know he'd had a lovely time, and I responded that I had a nice time as well. He told me I had the greatest tits he had ever seen, and I jokingly responded that he needed to get out more. So far, things were going great, and I spent the day doing all the usual Sunday activities: hanging out with the kids, shopping, doing meal prep, and figuring out the schedule for the coming week. That evening, I had an event at the high school, and while I was there milling around waiting for the start, I got a text from Matt.

It was a photo of his erect penis. I had just opened a photo of his erect penis in my kids' high school auditorium surrounded closely by people I knew.

And now, a word from our sponsor about dick pics.

A woman, no matter how attractive she thinks she may or may not be, cannot get out of any online dating experience without some working knowledge of the ins and outs of receiving dick pics. I for one never ask for them, though I am not a prude and have a healthy respect for the human form in all its glory. On those rare occasions where I hit it off with someone I am chatting with online, *and* we meet in person for one or more dates where there is actual intellectual and physical chemistry, the inevitable conversation about sex will arise and be discussed.

I know several women who have very specific rules about nude selfies (both taking and sending them), dick pics, and, of course, sex and dating in general. One friend asks for them on occasion. Another insists that any man who sends her an unsolicited dick pic is a monster. Still another, if she finds her suitor attractive, has been known to demand to see his cock very early on in the correspondence. If she likes what she sees, she will sext a virtual blow job in full detail before they even meet. In her words, "It sets the tone for the relationship." I have no judgment about anyone's sex life or stance on naked photography. Frankly, it's none of my affair. If the people I care about are safe, happy, and consenting, I say swing from the chandelier and live your best life.

I have received my fair share of dick pics, always unsolicited since I don't ask for them, but I don't have hard-and-fast rules about anything. This might be because I have enormous respect for the gay-male apps where dick pics are often part of the profile and can be unlocked by mutual likes and consent. I think they have us beat in both dating and sex in general. It's much more up-front and honest, and we heterosexuals should take a lesson.

And now, back to our originally scheduled prose.

I quickly shut off my phone after receiving the unexpected picture and slipped it into my purse. By the time I got home later that night and turned it on again, safely ensconced in my bedroom, there were a dozen more photos of his member taken from every possible angle, and maybe some new ones that he might want to add to the art form and photographic canon. It turns out, he might have been a tad insecure after all. I texted him that he was very impressive and that I had no doubt our next assignation would be a lot of fun, and that I was looking forward to seeing him again. I hoped that this reassurance would end the schlong show.

Hope springs eternal. The photos kept coming.

In the ensuing days, they came at random times. The first couple of times, I simply gave them the thumbs up, or made a joke about the other things in the photo like a little statue on his dresser in the background, or the color of his shower curtain, ignoring the main event completely hoping he would get the message. No matter how hard I rang his clue phone, he did not answer it or even seem to understand it was ringing. I finally told him that I understood that he might have felt awkward, but he need not, and I would like to see him again. I also very clearly

Dick Pics

asked him to stop sending me photos of his johnson at all hours of the day and night.

And then, he vanished.

At first, I just assumed he was busy. As the days stretched into a week, I realized that I would never hear from him again. I texted this message:

Am I to assume we have reached the ghosting stage of our relationship?

No response.

I waited a day and then texted:

Try adulting sometime. Who knows? You might like it.

I wasn't heartbroken or hurt by his juvenile behavior, but I was annoyed, mostly at myself. I had thought he had potential as a fun guy to date and had no illusions that he was my soul mate, as if I believed in such things anymore. His behavior reminded me of how my niece in the eighth grade described relationships between boys and girls. We now exist in an era where civility in communication is considered old-school and chivalry is relegated to stories from olden times. I wouldn't have minded it so much if I had at least enjoyed myself, but I didn't even get a lousy orgasm out of the experience. In addition to feeling detached from it all while it was happening because, unbeknownst to me, he was drunk, I also had to care for his fragile ego postcoital (if I can call it that) and for days afterward.

OVER DRINKS WITH A FEW FRIENDS, I told the tale of the Penis Prince, and my friends laughed their heads off as we sipped martinis. I like making them laugh. It's what I do. Making people laugh has always been a mechanism for me to avoid my pain. It is easier to entertain others than it is to feel decades of hurt. But then, as I sat with a group of women who I knew loved me and

My Year of Really Bad Dates

would never pass judgment on me, the sadness that came over me was so overwhelming that I could barely breathe despite the smile on my face. I panicked and told them I had to skedaddle early. I could still hear them laughing as I exited the restaurant and rushed to my car in time for the tears I couldn't control and the hyperventilating.

I knew that something was terribly wrong with me and that I needed help, but I couldn't seem to bring myself to ask. I didn't even know who or what to ask for at this stage. Most people assumed I was always fine because I projected that image. Alas, it was a mirage like a watery oasis in a desert that I wanted people to see. I was the opposite of fine. It felt like I had needs that not only had never been met but that I didn't even know existed. Despite my extensive vocabulary, I lacked the language skills that four-year-olds have when they need something.

I drove the few blocks home willing my breathing to stabilize before I walked through the door. I didn't want my children to see me in that state, but no matter how furiously I wiped my eyes, the tears kept coming. I pulled into my driveway and sat in my car until I could try to calm myself down, but one minute turned into ten, and even though my brain was telling my body to breathe normally and calm down, my body was in revolt and refused to listen to the signals it always obeyed.

I began to worry that I would have to spend the night in my car when my son appeared knocking at the window. He had pulled into the driveway on his bicycle from his dance class. I had no idea it was so late. There must be something to the idea of mothers having superpowers when they want to protect their children from something they don't want them to see because like magic, the tears dried, and my breathing stabilized. I got out of the car, and my son asked me why I was sitting in the car in the driveway. I told him that it was my only escape from the noise he and his sister made, and he laughed. Together, we walked his bike into the garage and went inside.

"Why are your eyes so red, Mommy?" he asked me.

"Allergies, I guess," I responded.

He looked at me like he wasn't buying it. "Go to the doctor. You have allergies all the time." He skipped down into the basement to finish his homework.

Kids are not stupid. He knew something was wrong, and I knew he knew, but I still said nothing. I did think that he might have been right. Maybe I should see a doctor. But which doctor? For what exactly? For now, I would soldier on and hope for the best. Unfortunately, rock bottom was inches away.

The Widower

IT WAS A COLD RAINY DAY at the end of April as I drove to my hometown of Buffalo, New York, for a reunion. I have been friends with Jim, Sean, and Kazim since I was fourteen years old. Sean and I attended the same high school while Kazim and Jim went to the other two schools in our district. We call ourselves the Angels, as in Charlie's, though we all fight over which one of us is Kate Jackson. (It's me, by the way. I am Kate Jackson.) In any group dynamic, there are roles. I am The Muscle and the only heterosexual; Jim, The Brains; Sean, The Looks; and Kazim, The Wild Card. We complement each other, argue, gossip, and generally support one another through careers, family, lovers, partners, and every other thing that life can throw in our paths.

I am fortunate to have many ride or dies and a best friend that I couldn't have dreamed up better if I tried, but the Angels are the most important friendship group I have ever had and likely ever will have. Perhaps the thing that bonds us is the trauma we share, each in our own way, or maybe it's where we are from, or the fact that we all speak fluent sarcasm and snark. The four of us share the unique characteristic of being detached from our emotions. We each have walls up for different reasons that we have a hard time lowering for anyone who hasn't known us for thirty or more years. I think the real reason is that long ago, we decided that the four of us were in a circle of trust without judgment.

The Widower

I need to amend that to say: no judgment about the things that matter. I could tell them that I had drunken sex with an entire Venezuelan soccer team on a public field and they would accept that as what I did last weekend. However, if my hair or outfit is not on point, I will hear the truth in no uncertain terms. The other important dynamic we have in common is that nobody expected much from us in our misspent youth, and we all went on to carve out unique niches in the fields of our choice and have been very successful.

Sean was invited to be the keynote speaker at a conference at the University of Buffalo, and he suggested I come and visit him when the conference ended since he lives in Paris and I only get to see him once a year or so. Hearing that I was coming, Jim decided to come in for the weekend from DC, and Kazim, upon hearing that the three of us would be together, decided that he would not be left behind and was coming from San Diego for the weekend as well.

This was an event. The Angels had not been together since before the pandemic, though we had seen each other individually or two at a time. It had been years since we were in Buffalo together. To commemorate such a momentous occasion, we decided to rent a house there and throw a party. Virtually everyone we still knew in Buffalo RSVP'd and we were expecting quite a turnout.

I thought that perhaps I would be able to talk to them about what was happening to me when we were all together. I could tell them about the crying jags that never ended, the Joe situation, the anxiety, and the terrible dreams that had me waking up sweating, panting, and, once, on the floor of my bedroom without being embarrassed. These were my people, my safe space. Surely, they would advise me well and help me through. I just had to get over that all-important hump of actually telling them.

My Year of Really Bad Dates

The night before I left for Buffalo, I set up a date with Kevin at a bar in Long Island City. He was very sweet and we had been talking for several weeks online and on the phone. He had two boys, similar in age to my children, and coincidentally, they were both in the arts like my kids. Also, he was a widower. I wasn't sure how long it had been exactly, and I was equally unsure of the right time to ask. Obviously, this man had been through it but retained a sense of humor and, from the little I knew, I liked him. He wanted a play-by-play of the weekend, and I promised to provide it in both text and pictures.

The weekend was fantastic. I saw people that I had not seen in decades, including my high school librarian and theater teacher. Several of my theater teacher's students finally got the chance to thank him in person for the tremendous influence he had on our lives, and Sean and I teared up a little that he cared enough about us to attend. We drank our weight in bourbon and our friend Meredith's signature cocktail (sharpie mustaches), laughed our heads off, and ate our hometown favorites while they vied for the attention of the sexy barista in the coffee shop around the corner from the rental that the boys referred to as "fun-size." For seventy-two hours, my troubles faded away, and I deluded myself into thinking that all was well and that I was now over the hump. I even foolishly complimented myself on not needing to talk to anyone and on getting over myself.

Getting over things has been a major saying and theme in my life. My parents were very big on getting over things with minimal intervention on their part. My in-laws were equally strong in this area, though their special realm of expertise was humiliating me. It was bad enough to be belittled and humiliated in their home in private, but the public humiliations over the years were on a different level entirely. On the few occasions when I tried to let them know that my husband's stepmother referring

The Widower

to me and my husband as "fucking asshole pieces of shit" at top volume in a crowded restaurant, in the lobby of a hotel, or on a city street upset me, their eyes would roll. I would be told to get over it while my father-in-law stood silently by like a tree stump and watched. I would be told to "be real," though I remain unsure what was meant by that phrase since in those moments, it was very real to me.

It happened over and over again, and the perpetrators even included my father-in-law's teenage children. My ex-husband's kid brother, eleven years his junior, at various times referred to me as an ingrate or a cunt. His aunt and uncle humiliated me at family events (and, once, in the museum where I was the CEO), screaming at my children or demanding payment for food I didn't eat. A few of their friends even joined the act. One in particular took special joy in making me look stupid at their parties or social gatherings. The first few times, I tried to let them know what was happening and was told to get over it. After that, I only complained once more toward the end of my marriage. That was met with an email in which my father-in-law told me that he was not interested in working on a relationship with me because he had to "fix his relationship with his son first." He went on to suggest that perhaps when that was settled, he would "revisit the issue." Today, my ex-husband communicates with him only through email every few months.

In 2017, a very famous Jewish film director and producer who was outed early in the #MeToo movement (which came just a hair too late for my career) was honored by the organization I was running. He sexually harassed me on multiple occasions. Once in our offices in New York, and later at his house in Los Angeles during the middle of a party when he asked me to come upstairs to look at something cool in his bedroom.

"I'm not going to your bedroom," I told him.

He smiled. "You are so my type though: cute Jewish girl next door."

"Why me?" I asked. "There are three hundred women at this party, and all of them are model-hot. Also, the woman calling herself your fiancée and wearing a diamond ring the size of my head is twenty feet away." He just laughed. Luckily, I ran into an old friend, and he got me out of there at that moment.

I shakily shared this with my board after our event, during which he'd put his hand on my ass while telling me he'd love to fuck me as my then husband stood mere feet away. The response from the all-white male board members over sixty who were present for this executive committee meeting was laughter. Then they told me it wasn't a big deal and I should get over it. After all, the board chair pointed out, nothing bad happened, and we raised $1 million in a night!

I have been getting over things quietly since birth without apology or acknowledgment, and at almost fifty, I might have Stockholm syndrome. I take pride in shoving it all down and getting over it, as though this somehow makes me superior instead of completely unhinged and unhealthy.

ON MY LAST MORNING IN BUFFALO, I woke up hungover and missing Joe. I had not heard from him in a month, and against my better judgment, I texted him. He responded immediately and seemed delighted to hear from me. Joe was originally from Toronto, and since Buffalo is a mere ninety minutes away, I was reminded of how we used to reminisce about our childhoods, how we lived close together, and our mutual love of butter tarts (don't ask but trust me, they are as delicious as they sound). We Buffalonians often joke that Toronto is our largest suburb, though we are the inferior city. I told him I had been through his Canadian

The Widower

homeland and was thinking of him. He told me he missed me too and thought of me all the time. I told him that he should come home in that case, and we texted back and forth for a while until it was time for me to hit the road. We agreed to talk soon, and I wondered if he was starting to regret his decision to leave me. I wanted him to regret it because I wanted someone to feel as bad as I did.

I spent the morning saying goodbye to my favorite people, and then Meredith and I went to Wegmans so I could pick up some snacks and a sub sandwich for the road. While we perused the store, she shared with me that she was struggling hard, and we both cried in the potato chip aisle. I marveled at her ability to be open with me and I wanted to tell her what was going on with me too, but of course, I only glazed over the surface. I assured her I was fine, made a joke, and focused my attention back on her story, which is how I always deflect attention from myself when I am uncomfortable.

I dropped her at the airport on my way out of town and headed out for the seven-hour drive home. It was pouring rain, which made the drive nine and a half hours long. The weather gave me a lot of quiet time to think. I realized for the first time that my refusal to talk about my pain or ask for support was selfish, not selfless. How can the people who love me the most know me unless they know the full picture about me? How can I be a true friend to anyone if I am withholding and dishonest about my own life? I vowed on that drive that the next time someone asked me how I was, I would share that I was struggling and needed some help. The thought never crossed my mind that I could just pick up a phone and call or text someone, but Rome wasn't built in a day, and neither would I be rebuilt in a short period. I viewed my decision as progress and a great leap forward.

When I staggered in from the downpour and the horrendous traffic, the house was wrecked. The kids were at one another's

My Year of Really Bad Dates

throats, and my ex-husband, who was supposed to be watching them, was nowhere to be found. They weren't babies, but they weren't grown either. Someone needed to check in on them occasionally lest their idle hands do the devil's work while they are unsupervised for eight hours. They had not eaten and there was no food in the house, so I threw together a meal like MacGyver out of eggs and stale bread before I finally sank into a hot bath and tried to unkink myself from the long drive. As I lounged in the bathtub, I picked up my phone and saw that Joe had texted me, as he always used to, to make sure I had arrived home safely.

Then, I decided to ruin a perfectly good tub by looking at his social media.

There was a photo montage of his arrival at the Phoenix airport, surrounded by his family and his blond real estate agent. I was transfixed by her appearance, and I studied it like I was looking at a document to add to an archive, examining her image from every possible angle. She was not unattractive, but she was no supermodel either. A rabbit hole opened, and I looked at her Facebook page. It was filled with trite quotes, images of cheap chardonnay, and trays of pepperoni she put together to celebrate #livingherbestlife, #newbeginnings, and #lovewhatyoudo.

I hate those sayings. Whenever Lynn and I are in HomeGoods picking up something, we love to read these silly life-affirming sayings off cheap throw pillows or on signs meant to be hung in suburban powder rooms or kitchens. We also enjoy reading cheesy greeting cards about love and friendship when we are in CVS. We have been engaged in this hobby for thirty years now, and it is still one of our favorite things we do together.

"When God closes a door, he opens a window," I called to her from the bathroom accessories at Bed Bath & Beyond one Sunday afternoon.

The Widower

"There's nothing you can't achieve if you believe in yourself!" Lynn yelled to me once from the "Friendship" section of the card display at CVS on a rainy Wednesday night, after we'd snuck out of the house for a few hours to grab a drink and buy garbage bags, a small respite from the kids.

What sent me over the precipice looking at her Facebook page were the unironic videos she'd posted from her car where she discussed how much she loves touring median-priced suburban homes in the Phoenix area. I sent them to my girlfriend Leah, who is a high-end real estate agent in New York. She texted back that the videos were amazing and exactly what *not* to do if anyone wants to be taken seriously in her business. The blond's voice grated on my nerves, and there was a vacant quality to her face and eyes like there was nothing behind the façade. The Joe I knew was whip-smart and one of the most intellectually curious men I'd ever met. We talked about politics, God, death, travel, and every other subject, and I couldn't fathom how he was getting through the day on platitudes, discussions of interest rates, and cheap chardonnay—which he doesn't drink.

She also was a mother. I saw a photo of her with her daughter, whom she had taken to some real estate event. I didn't like her, but I got it. Her options, it seemed, were more limited than mine. Joe had money, personality, and looks. I saw why she jumped at the chance to date him; he provided her with financial stability that she couldn't provide for herself. And on his end, she kept him company while he started a new life. Up until that moment, I had never stalked an ex on social media, and I'm not sure what compelled me to do it then, but thankfully, just before I drowned myself, I came to my senses, shut off my phone, and made a promise to my inner soul that I would never do that again. I didn't feel good exactly, but I wasn't distraught either.

My Year of Really Bad Dates

THE NEXT NIGHT WAS MY date with Kevin. We met in a terrific dive bar in Long Island City, and from the minute he walked up to the door, I liked him. We took a little booth inside the dark bar, so dark that I could barely see my hand in front of my face. The cocktail menu was fabulous, and we both needed phone flashlights to read it and select our choices. The conversation flowed from the first, and I found myself enjoying being on a date for the first time in a long time. I felt pretty and flirty, and we made one another laugh. He even stood up when I went to use the bathroom, like a real live gentleman.

After two drinks, I finally got up the courage to ask him about the death of his wife. He took a deep breath and told me the story of how, a week shy of one year ago, she had an aneurysm right in front of him and died in their apartment. Their marriage had been a difficult one, and he told me they had not been intimate in more than five years. They had begun the early process of divorce before she died, but they were high school sweethearts, and her sudden and unexpected loss was devastating.

He assured me that he was ready to start his life anew and that he had been out a few times but hadn't clicked with anyone until he met me. I smiled at him on the outside, but on the inside, my heart sank. I could tell by the way he shared his story that within, he was still a disaster. He didn't have a clue who he was alone as a single man, or what he wanted in a relationship since he had only had one in the entirety of his life. I could tell he desperately wanted to find the love of his life and be done with it, but he was missing some steps in between. His words said he was ready, but his eyes said something much different.

The date lasted four hours and we did it all: We laughed, we cried, and we held hands on the way to my car. He kissed

The Widower

me gently and perfectly. It was the best first date I'd had all year, and as I pulled away, I knew I would never see him again. I went through the motions of texting him that I had a lovely time and would like to see him again. He texted back the same. We went back and forth the week of the anniversary of his wife's death, and the inevitable happened. He went radio silent. I checked in with him a week later, and he told me he and his boys were struggling. I sent him a nice message every few days and he always responded quickly, but I could tell that he had already drifted away into his sea of self-doubt, survivor's guilt, and fear.

After two weeks of back-and-forth, I texted him that I liked him a lot but that I didn't think we were a match. I was looking for something specific, and he wasn't sure what he was looking for at all. A few hours later, he agreed with me but expressed sadness that I came along too soon. We agreed to check in six months down the line, just to say hello and see how the other was getting along. I was grateful for the good date, but I could also feel myself sinking further into the abyss, and that was becoming more problematic with each passing day. I was starting to wonder how long I could live like that if nothing changed, and it occurred to me that if nothing did, I was going to die young.

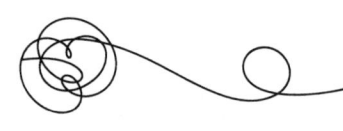

The Most Rigid Man in New York

I'D PROMISED MYSELF THAT THE NEXT TIME someone asked how I was, I would be honest and ask for help. A few weeks after I made that vow, my girlfriend Leah called.

I hadn't heard from her in several weeks, and when her name popped up, I automatically smiled. Externally, Leah is my opposite. She is a real estate agent. These days, I hate real estate agents, but she is my one exception. She is a lover of makeup, plastic surgery, anything New Age, and decorative nails, all things I normally think are ridiculous. The last time we went out to dinner, she showed up with what looked like a jewel-encrusted magic wand. I asked her if it was for her son or daughter's school play, but she laughed and told me it was exactly what it looked like: a magic wand that had been treated by a Reiki expert. Then she waved it over my head while I laughed. She assured me it held power.

Internally, Leah is my soul mate. We crack each other up, she is incredibly smart and savvy, and she is an exceptional professional who takes her work, her clients, and her life very seriously. Like me, she tends toward sarcasm and workaholism. She is never shy to express her real opinions or feelings. She is civic-minded, knows everyone in town, and is self-made. Being around her is always a good time. The phone call went like this:

The Most Rigid Man in New York

"*Dude!* You have been popping into my head all week. I know something is going on with you. What is up?" Leah asked.

Normally, this was my cue to say that I was fine. Everything was fine. But everything was not fine, and I began to hate the word *fine*. My father used to tell me that whenever I used that word, he knew I was full of shit. He wasn't a tactful man, a trait that I inherited from him, but he was not wrong in this instance. I remembered the promise I'd made to myself that the next time someone asked me how I was, I would tell them the truth and ask for help.

So I replied, "Well, I'm okay. I'm not great."

That was the best I could do, and it felt lame coming out of my mouth. Luckily, she knew me well enough to realize I was full of shit.

"Whatever, dude. Let's get together this weekend so we can talk for real. Brunch Saturday?"

We planned to meet at my favorite lunch spot, and something about putting it on my calendar made me feel lighter and better. I even decided that no matter what, I was going to enjoy the two dates that I had scheduled that week. I was meeting the first tonight at a club in Midtown for a drink on the roof deck, which had just opened for the season, and I was looking forward to feeling the air on my skin while I drank my favorite cocktail outside.

He was waiting for me when I arrived, and we ascended to the roof together. He was neatly dressed, knife creased in fact, and I couldn't believe he had come so perfectly straight from a full day of work in an office. He was very tall and had a nondescript but kind face, round and flat, with a thatch of neatly combed dark hair. He was the kind of man who is hard to describe even moments after you leave him, but pleasant enough. I could tell he was shy, but I couldn't get a read on him. We sat down at a

My Year of Really Bad Dates

sweet little table right in the center and went through the cocktail menu.

I think you can tell a lot about a person by how they order a drink. First, both sexes need to pass the important hurdle of baseline civility. Would that this would be obvious, but sadly, I have witnessed and heard tell of both men and women behaving like fools toward waitstaff and servers in restaurants and bars. It is appalling behavior to mistreat anyone in the service industry. It's not about being a Karen; it's about being a human and treating people decently. Second, in my experience, you can tell a lot about a man by what he orders and how he drinks. My date passed the first test with flying colors but seemed confused by the drink menu and ordered a cola. For a minute I panicked and wondered if I'd brought someone sober to a bar who was too polite to let me know that he doesn't drink, but afterward, he admitted that he only ever ordered one kind of alcoholic beverage, a vodka and soda, and he didn't see it on the menu. When the waiter came over again, he asked for whatever was closest to vodka and soda, and the waiter told him he was happy to just bring him one. It's a bar. They can make any drink, and it confused me that a fifty-two-year-old man did not understand this concept.

I soon learned why.

As we sipped our beverages, he told me he'd lived in the same apartment since he was twenty-three, a rent-stabilized place he moved into when his uncle died. This is not uncommon in New York City, where people try to hang on to real estate lightning such as this when it strikes. What is not common is that he went on to explain that the furniture was the same as it was when his uncle moved in. In 1967. He also told me he wore the same clothes every day to the office, owning seven of the same work shirts in different colors and three pairs of work pants, which he rotated daily and took to the cleaners every ten days. I asked him what

The Most Rigid Man in New York

he wore on weekends and learned that he had four sweatshirts, three sweaters, and a dozen of the same T-shirts in assorted colors. Order and simplicity, he explained to me, are very important for living a successful life. He asked me why women needed more than three pairs of shoes when sneakers, everyday shoes, and a pair of black heels for date night should be sufficient. He also asked me about handbags and why a woman would need more than two, a black and a white, since "those two colors go with everything." He went on to let me know he thought most women buy shoes, bags, jewelry, and clothes to impress men, but they shouldn't because men don't care about such things. He asked me my thoughts on the subject.

I already knew there was no way we were a match. My closet would likely give him heart palpitations. Until I was forty-four years old, I had six pairs of shoes and four handbags. My feet are very wide and long; my father used to refer to them as "big fat loppers" when he was forced to take me shoe shopping once a year. What teenage girl doesn't want a body part of hers referred to that way, after all? Shoe shopping was always a traumatic experience for me, and I avoided it whenever possible, preferring to run into a Payless when I was desperate, buying the first pair that didn't cripple me when I put them on. Spending money on myself always seemed indulgent since I rarely had disposable income and I felt the money was better spent on my kids.

A few years ago, I decided to change my relationship with money and allow myself a few nice things. I'm no Imelda Marcos, but I now own several pairs of designer shoes and handbags.

As I was organizing my thoughts in a way that didn't make me sound judgmental or shallow, he mercifully changed the subject and asked me what I like to do for fun. I told him I love the water, so any kind of lake, beach, or ocean activity is for me, plus museums and the other things I had listed on my profile. I asked

My Year of Really Bad Dates

him what he liked to do for fun since his profile was sparse in this area, and he told me he had very few hobbies. He mostly liked to work, come home, have one vodka and soda, and then watch reruns of *Cops* until he fell asleep, at exactly 10:15 each evening. This amazed me. I asked him how he went to sleep at precisely that time each night (including weekends), and he showed me an app on his phone connected to a contraption on his wrist that tracked his sleep. He got the same amount every night. This tracked, given that he seemed to do everything the same every single day of his life. He'd already told me he drank one cup of coffee in the morning and half of a cup of decaf at 1:15 each afternoon. He also ate the same lunch every day at the same diner around the corner from his office. I asked him if he ever deviated from any aspect of his schedule. He did not. It was like dating Jack Nicholson in *As Good as It Gets*.

Thirty-one minutes into the date, I took a new path. The older I get, the more I realize that I am pained the most when my time, not my money, is wasted. I think most people my age feel the same way, and I didn't want to waste his time either. We were finishing our first round when I decided to be honest with him and tell him outright that he was a nice man, but we were not a match. He seemed stunned. In a very loud voice, he asked me why I felt that way, and that he thought I should give him more of a chance because he was a great guy. His voice rose with each syllable. I should have kept my mouth shut, endured the rest of the date, and gone home to watch *The Mary Tyler Moore Show*, but it was too late. I very calmly told him that I just didn't think our personalities would match up and that I had a fondness for all the things he claimed not to like or understand, like extra shoes, different kinds of booze and food, and a schedule that wavers from day to day. I blamed myself and I told him I was likely too effuse and scattered for a man like him.

The Most Rigid Man in New York

He stood up and self-righteously agreed with me. He stormed off, leaving me the check, but not before he very loudly told me I was a materialistic, selfish jerk who didn't know a good man when she met one and didn't deserve him. I suddenly realized that outside of one elderly couple sipping martinis, I was the only woman on the roof deck. Everyone else was a white man, about my date's age, and they were all staring at me. I don't know how or why I ended up at a middle-aged white-guy convention on that roof deck, but there I was. To these men, I must have represented every awful woman and date they'd ever had, and it showed in the judgment and disdain on their faces. If I stayed for one more minute, I worried, they might declare me a witch and bring me to the inquisitor waiting down below in the kitchen to burn me.

I did the only thing I could, which was to leave what we owed plus a huge tip and slink out as quickly as possible. It had felt good to sit outside though. As much as I hate trite, pithy expressions and hashtags, I couldn't help but giggle as I responded to a text message from a girlfriend asking me how my date went. I simply texted back *#winning*. It felt appropriate for the occasion. Besides, I had another date later in the week. That one couldn't be as bad, right?

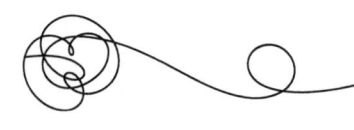

Tie Me Up, Get Me Outta Here

MAY MEANS SPRING IS IN FULL SWING in New York. It is my favorite season and by far the shortest. I love wearing a sweater or light jacket and wandering around the city between errands and meetings. I love riding my bike and opening the windows when I sleep. There is always a renewed sense of hope when the daffodils and peonies start popping up around my neighborhood. Despite the abysmal fall and winter, I couldn't help but feel good about the future as the days got longer with summer and my fiftieth birthday right around the corner. Soon, my daughter would graduate from high school, and it looked as though my son might pass geometry. In a few short months, I would be fifty. I was cautiously optimistic, though the New York Jew in me still knew that things could always get worse. After all, there was always a pile of shoes waiting to be dropped on my head from a great height.

MY FRIEND LEAH AND I met for brunch on a beautiful Saturday morning, and as soon as we sat down, she grabbed my hand and asked me what the hell was going on with me. It all came tumbling out, and I started to explain why I was responsible for every awful thing that had occurred over the last five years. Leah stopped me mid-sentence. It was no accident that she was the

Tie Me Up, Get Me Outta Here

one I chose to spill my guts to, mainly because like me, she is a linear thinker who is solution-oriented, and I knew she wouldn't let me wallow for very long.

She didn't. Not only could I not wallow, but she also didn't even let me dip a toe in the wading pool of self-pity that I had been submerged in for months. In a heartbeat, she pulled out her phone, and within seconds, I had text messages from her containing the contact information for two people she swore would help me: a psychic/astrologer and a psychiatrist.

I wasn't sure about the star-reading psychic. It made me nervous, partly because in my formative years, I was raised in a deeply religious community that frowned on that sort of thing, but also because I spent years making fun of Dionne Warwick's Psychic Friends Network and it seemed hypocritical of me to consult one now. But Leah insisted that I at least call him to make an appointment because, in her words, it would be "life-changing."

The psychiatrist also gave me pause. I've spent huge chunks of my life in therapy, and in my experience, I have only ever had one therapist who I think made a difference. My ex-husband loved the process of therapy. Outcomes never interested him much, but therapy itself made him hot. I put him through graduate school to become a therapist, and while I am told he is excellent at what he does, in real life outside of his practice, his adulting skills are nonexistent and he can never seem to find his ass with his two hands. As the saying goes, the shoemaker never has shoes. (It's always about the shoes.) The idea of starting at the top all over again with a new therapist made me itchy and I broke out into a sweat, but Leah saw this and stopped my negative monologue before it started.

She said this therapy, Rapid Transformational Therapy, or RTT, was different . . . a combination of hypnosis, talk therapy, and coaching on only one issue over a month. I was skeptical.

My Year of Really Bad Dates

I had never been hypnotized, and I didn't want to cluck like a chicken if someone used the trigger word. She laughed, called me weird, and made me promise to make an appointment as soon as I got home. She also told me that she would call the doctor herself, and if I didn't make the appointment, she would.

The act of coming clean to a friend was liberating, even though I had reservations. I had no illusions that magic-bullet hypnoses would change any aspect of my life or that a psychic would predict my future successes or failures, but none of my lame attempts at helping myself had worked, and something needed to change. Bob Proctor, a renowned Canadian writer, once famously said, "If you want to change your life, then change your life."

This statement seems simple, but it's loaded. Most people don't ever change their lives. They playact at it, but they only change the set, like the Christmas windows at Macy's. They leave partners and places, jobs, and even religions thinking themselves radical, but the truth is, as Bob so eloquently implied, the real work is much harder. It is only an internal change that can cause a seismic shift, and that is much too scary for most people. It's why we find ourselves replaying our old relationships or staying in professions that we don't love. It's why we as a species continue to hate one another. The internal work is no joke. It's painful and difficult, and most people would rather sleep through life than live it. Most people are like the zombies on *The Walking Dead*. They are not living but going through the physical motions of living: careening from day to day, place to place, surviving off the scraps they find or are given.

I'd spent decades in a zombie state, living, yet not, subsisting, not thriving. I wanted to thrive now. The self-help programs, multilevel marketing companies, and gurus that promote goal-setting and quick-fix life hacks in a short period are businesses. There is

Tie Me Up, Get Me Outta Here

no quick fix. The work takes a lifetime, and anyone who offers you a shortcut also likely has a bridge in Brooklyn to sell. I left a message for the therapist when I got home, and then I got ready for my date.

ON PAPER, YUVAL COULD HAVE BEEN my perfect match. An Israeli surgeon, he was born and raised on a kibbutz in the middle of the country but abandoned religion in favor of culture and peoplehood. Yuval hated Bibi more than I did and found the Likud political party he grew up endorsing had morphed into a hellacious right-wing party of religious fanatics. He seemed to have a good sense of humor from our text banter and exchanges, and when we spoke on the phone, he was gentle and soft-spoken but quick-witted and easygoing. He suggested that we meet at the oyster bar in Grand Central Station, which I have found to be an iconic, casual, and good place for a first date, especially during happy hour. Even after I applied the dating math algorithm in my head, which aged him five years and decreased his height by four inches, he was still someone I'd date.

I texted him when I arrived at the bar, and he was already there, sitting at the counter nursing a beer. He looked calm and exactly like his photographs. He was the exact height listed in his profile, and I was betting that he was honest about his age as well. He was dressed perfectly; his pants were knife creased and his designer shirt had the look of being casually slung across his back. He was wearing an enormous Rolex. The whole look was immaculate and meant to convey success and a relaxed unpretentiousness. I momentarily forgot two important details about Israeli men. The first is that they can be vain. Second, they are known for their brutal candor when it comes to themselves and what they think of others.

My Year of Really Bad Dates

I sat down next to him, and we started up a flowing, easy conversation in a mixture of Hebrew and English, which seemed to tickle him. Like all Israelis, he seemed baffled that I spoke Hebrew as well as I did though I am not Israeli. I ordered my usual pinot noir, and he ordered a bunch of food. I felt warm and relaxed as our conversation naturally unfolded. We had a lot in common, from our political beliefs to our aesthetics. He too had recently seen the Mayan show at the Met and loved it, and we both thought that *Monster: The Jeffrey Dahmer Story* was one of the best things we had ever seen on television. The more we chatted, the more comfortable I felt, which had not been the case in many moons. All the anxiety and sadness that had been plaguing me faded away temporarily, and I found myself getting lost in the conversation, the way your troubles fade away when you're watching a great movie or reading a fantastic book.

About thirty-five minutes into the date, he set his second beer down on the counter of the bar with a thud, turned his full body toward me, and said, "*Tachlis?*"

This is a quintessentially Jewish moment. The word *tachlis* roughly translates to the phrase "Let's get down to brass tacks."

In other words, Yuval wanted to get straight to the point. This brings me to a third important detail about Israeli men, which is the absence of embarrassment or shame when discussing anything deeply personal with a virtual stranger, from the amount of money they earn to their most recent bathroom habits. After a lifetime of dealing with Israeli men, and Israelis in general, I was prepared for almost anything, so I answered, "*Betach*," which roughly translates to "Of course." It turned out, I was unprepared for this particular brass tack.

He told me that he thought I was a beautiful, intelligent woman and would very much like me to be his fourth.

Tie Me Up, Get Me Outta Here

I wondered if he was confused about my preferences. I am not polyamorous. I have no judgment about those who are, but I am not. My ex-husband and I experimented with an open marriage the last few years we were together. It was our last attempt at meeting one another's needs since I couldn't take care of him any longer, and he had never been interested in meeting my needs from day one, mostly because he was unwell so much of the time. At first, when my ex suggested it, my feelings were hurt, but the more I thought about it, the more appealing the idea became. I wanted to feel attractive and be taken out on a nice date occasionally. I wanted to take a vacation once a year and maybe even engage in a hobby with my partner. And I wanted to please my husband and make my marriage work. He wanted sex with other women. I got it. We met when we were nineteen and started dating when I was twenty-one. Neither of us is a particularly jealous person. We had been together so long that we were both secure in our relationship. In my profile, I did write that I had experimented with all kinds of dynamics in relationships, including polyamory and open relationships, but that I was all through with that now and was looking for someone to share my life with. Perhaps Yuval hadn't read to the end.

Before I had a chance to explain or inquire further, Yuval told me that I would be his ideal fourth sexual partner and went on to say that he wasn't interested in an actual relationship, just sex, because women were too demanding of his time and money. Furthermore, he explained that he had recently developed an interest in a new hobby called *Shibari* and would like to experiment on me. He actually used the word *experiment*, like the Jewish Mengele.

Shibari is a contemporary form of rope bondage that originated in Japan. According to Rabbi Google, *Shibari* is "a great way to bring healthy communication, trust, and spice into your bedroom game, no matter how kinky you are on the BDSM spectrum."

I'd heard of this practice before and seen some photos at a gallery show of complicated knots and multiple ropes that fully restrain a person, the act of restraining and being restrained a sexual turn-on for some people. I have no judgment or issue with this practice in theory if I'm in a relationship with someone I trust. But I'd known this man for less than an hour. I usually like to start with a few dates and engage in a sexual relationship with someone before I head into Kinkville, if I ever decide to head there with someone at all. Having this man tie me to his radiator did not appeal to me in the least.

Before I had the chance to answer again, he further explained that four was his ideal number of women to fuck because he got bored easily and women in general bored him after a time. He smiled as he shared this tidbit of how dull he found my gender and expressed how refreshing it was that he could talk to me so candidly because, obviously, I understood him. It confused me how he'd discerned that I got him, outside of our shared religious and cultural backgrounds, but he went on to talk about his stable in detail (he actually used the word *stable*). His stable of women had been perfectly arrayed until an unfortunate accident in which he dislocated the shoulder of his last fourth. She had no name, mind you. Just a number. She was fourth. His disregard for human beings reminded me of a story I'd heard from a producer on the hit television series *Roseanne* in the nineties. She hired and fired writers at such an alarming rate that she didn't want to bother learning their names. She suggested instead that in meetings, they wear numbers pinned to their shirts so she could just yell out to number three that their script sucked.

I have dislocated my shoulder before. Two years ago, due to a series of very poor life choices involving wheelie shoes, a global pandemic that caused some delusional thinking, an ex-husband who would walk into my house at all hours of the day and night, and a crack in the bike path behind my house. I broke my ankle in three places and dislocated my shoulder at the same time in one spectacular fall. I spent almost three months immobile in bed and have nine pins and a plate in my ankle because of a ten-minute poor life choice. The pain of both dislocating and then relocating my shoulder haunts me. It was possibly the worst pain I have ever experienced, and I gave birth to two ten-pound babies without anesthesia. The noise I heard emerge from myself when they put my shoulder back into its socket with a nauseating crack is something I never care to revisit.

As I tried to figure out how to answer him, he finished his pitch to me with, "You won't have to worry about dislocations anymore, though. I got a blow-up doll and I've been practicing a lot on that. It bends like a real girl!"

It dawned on me that there were no words to respond to his last statement. I was now picturing an accomplished surgeon with his knee on the back of a life-sized rubber doll trying to force its lifeless arm backward at an awkward angle so he could practice tying a Windsor knot. I think I saw something like this on an episode of *20/20*. It could have been *48 Hours*. Come to think of it, I'm pretty sure it was *Dateline*. There was something deeply unsettling about the man I was sitting next to, and my gut was telling me to leave immediately. I didn't feel like I was in imminent danger; it's just that I no longer wanted to be in his presence. I could not unsee the image I had created of him wrestling a plastic female form into submission in practice for the next time he had a real live girl in front of him. This wasn't about arousal or pleasure or taking care of a partner. This was about power, and it gave me the creeps.

My Year of Really Bad Dates

I excused myself to go to the bathroom and exited through the little-known back way out of the oyster bar, which leads right into the tunnel toward the Metro-North line at Grand Central Station. As I stood up, he kindly told me, "You don't have to answer me tonight. You should think about it for a while."

I am convinced that whoever designed the oyster bar made that exit an escape for women just like me, and I was eternally grateful to the architect. I wound my way through the tunnel and back to the food hall in the station. After that encounter, I deserved a banana pudding from Magnolia Bakery, and by some miracle, there was no line. From there, I descended the long escalator to the Long Island Rail Road section of the station, which had just opened after years of construction. It was only the second time I'd taken that line home. The trains are brand-new ones with comfy seats, nicer lighting, and outlets to charge your phone at every seat. It was quiet because I managed to avoid both rush hour after work and rush hour after a night in the city.

I took up a whole bench usually meant for three and spread out in the empty car as the train pulled away. The first perfect spoonful of the pudding hit my tongue and I felt my body release with the treat. As I put in my earbuds and listened to Bonnie Raitt's husky, soothing voice croon "Angel from Montgomery," I took stock of my situation.

I'd had the worst luck since people began what we refer to as modern dating. It couldn't sink any lower, I thought, unless, of course, I wound up the subject of a *Dateline* special. I could hear Keith Morrison's masculine voice setting the scene: "Her life was going along fine until she met the doctor who wanted to dislocate her entire body and pack it away in a set of Louis Vuitton luggage."

I went into the dating app on my phone and checked when my subscription ran out. Crap. I saw that I was paid through July. I turned off the notifications so that when someone sent me a

Tie Me Up, Get Me Outta Here

message, I wouldn't know unless I voluntarily opened the app. I also deleted the app from my home screen so that I would have to go to the website to look. It was a huge relief. I'd be damned if my name became associated with forty-eight minutes of exploitive television with the words *murder*, *night*, or *vanish* in the title. I was flooded with relief in the knowledge that even though I would die alone with a cat that I hated, I would have at least escaped that humiliation.

As the train hurtled me toward home, I got a text from my daughter. She had failed her driving test for the fourth time. She went on in a second text to say it was not her fault because her instructor wasn't clear in the directions. I'd suggested on multiple occasions that she should take some lessons from a person who was not related to her, but my ex-husband told me that was stupid, and that I should stay out of it, so I ignored the message. I then noticed that I had a voicemail. It was the psychiatrist Leah had recommended. I took it as a sign and made a note to call her back the following day.

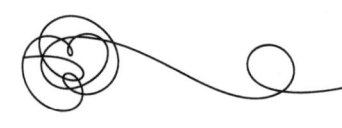

Flake
Before Meeting

AFTER AN INITIAL CONVERSATION with Dr. Z on the phone, I set up an appointment to meet in her office the following week. There was a feeling of apprehension about starting therapy again, but the previous day, I had to force myself to get up in the morning, and all day long, the only thing I wanted was to get back into bed. That couldn't be good.

The last time I saw Joe, in his car on that dreary March morning, I'd encouraged him to find a therapist once he moved to Phoenix so that he could figure out why he blew up his life, why he was leaving the woman he loved for a woman he didn't, and why, in general, he always settled when it came to women, though he wouldn't settle for anything else in his life. He told me in no uncertain terms that he would not seek therapy and then hit me with a series of platitudes he'd picked up from the multi-level marketing self-improvement program he was now devoted to, which had seemingly turned his once-keen mind into tapioca. He told me that we (I guess he meant the royal *we*, as in humanity) are our choices and that for him to stay in integrity, he had to follow through on the commitment he'd made to himself to see if he could conquer his biggest fear. I'm not sure how someone can stay inside an amorphous noun, but that moment didn't feel ripe for an English lesson. I also somehow knew at that moment that

Flake Before Meeting

I was being hypocritical by suggesting something that I didn't want for myself but likely needed even more than he did.

I had a long conversation with my agent about my novel, which had been on submission for months. Everything in publishing now moves at a glacial pace, though he was convinced the book would sell and assured me that it was terrific. I took a yoga class, wrote two thousand new words on my latest project, and in general was feeling productive—until I broke for lunch and looked through my phone. I only look through my phone at the top of each hour, when my online writing sprint group breaks for ten minutes, or when I eat lunch. Cute-screenwriter Paul, my writing buddy and pretend love interest I'd been flirting with for two years but who lived in Tucson (what is it with men wanting to live in that godforsaken place?) once told me that the phone blocks the creative process and encouraged me to not look at it until I've been up and working for an hour. I can't always do this since my children sometimes text me emergency messages like:

I forgot _____. If you don't drop it off at school by ten I'll _____ [insert the words *die, fail,* or *be in trouble*].

But mostly, his advice was spot-on and life-changing. My creativity only lives if the sun shines anyway. By five in the afternoon, every impulse of originality and all my synapses slowly drain off any intellectual energy.

I hadn't opened the dating app since my half-date with Dr. Slip Knot the week before. Against my better judgment, and because I had nothing but junk in my email, I double-clicked to see what fresh hell awaited me, but I was also hopeful that there was at least one interesting man left in the world. I missed having some male energy in my daily life, and since I was living like a nun, I would've been satisfied with just exchanging some fun text messages. I still responded to text messages from Joe now and then, but I no longer initiated them, which I decided was progress. In our last exchange, he shared with me that he loved his real estate agent deeply but differently from the ways that he loved me deeply. His message made me gag because I knew somewhere deep down he was lying both to me and to himself.

There, waiting in my inbox, was a series of notes from men who looked decent and sounded (one sent me a voice text) like they were looking for something similar to what I was seeking. Two of the five that had messaged me were the same type I always go for: tall, funny, handsome, job-holding, and, at least initially, seemingly smart enough to hold a decent conversation. I sent a note back to the two I liked. I also responded to the other three with a message that I didn't think we were a good match. I do that with everyone who reaches out to me, unless they call me *honey*, or *dear*, or say something completely gross and sexual in the first sentence. I think it is the kind thing to do, and I try to live by the do-unto-others principle.

After a couple of hours of work, I checked my phone again and was surprised to see that the two I liked had both replied. It rarely happens that the man you like likes you back on an app so quickly, let alone two in one day. In addition to writing those two thousand words, catching up on my bills, and, for a change, buying all the ingredients I needed to make dinner that evening in one trip, I'd hit the dating-math lottery. It was one of those rare moments where one plus one really equaled two. I started chats with both.

The first was Brent. He was adorable and left me a very cute voice text as a message of introduction. His voice was soothing and he was funny with a splash of irony and sarcasm in just the right places. By the end of the week, we were leaving one another voicemails on the app a few times a day and we graduated to talking on the phone. He taught religion and ethics, and we loved the same movies, food, alcohol, and outdoor activities. We had

Flake Before Meeting

the same taste in books as well, which is the holy grail of dating anyone, online or otherwise. By week two, we were texting back and forth daily and talking on the phone most evenings. We finally decided to meet for lunch later that week, and I was excited to meet him in person.

When I woke up that morning at six thirty, I found the following text message:

Not going to be able to make it today. At my father's again all night. I'll ttyl and explain more. I can't right now.

Of course, I was disappointed, but there was something important and difficult happening in his life. I responded:

Oh no. I hope you and your family are all right. Talk to you soon.

That evening as I was cooking dinner, I got another text message from him.

Hey. This is gonna be my whole summer with this fucking guy, I just know it. Too much to text. Exhausted.

I asked him if he wanted to talk later when I was done making dinner.

Maybe. Go do your thing.

Then nothing.

In our previous text messages, he'd told me he had a great feeling about me, and that he was more into me than he had remembered ever being. We had great banter and laughed a lot when we spoke on the phone. He was sweet, charming, attentive, and all the things I'd want in a man to date, but he disappeared with no explanation and without a trace. The great irony was that he listed the most important quality that he was looking for as "consistency." I tried to reach out to him a few times but received no response.

I spoke to my girlfriend Celia, the therapist who lives in Los Angeles. We have been friends since we were fourteen and were in the same boat. Her boyfriend left her a few months before Joe ended things with me. At least Joe had the decency to tell me to my face the numerous times he ended our relationship. Her boyfriend broke up with her in an email, which I think is worse. She and I were both deep in the throes of online dating. Too deep. We traded awful profiles, me sending her my Idi Amin look-alike whose opening line to me was:

You look like a sexy bitch.

She sent me a potential mate who was wearing an Elizabethan collar and monocle in his profile picture. We were on the same page with unsolicited dick pics and inappropriate messages we sometimes received from potential gentleman callers.

Her take was that Brent either was married and was discovered, found someone "better," or legitimately had a life-altering family tragedy to deal with, though she was dubious about the third option. Even if, God forbid, some terrible fate had befallen him, he should have at least sent me a farewell text message or, at the very least, an apology. I was annoyed by his disappearance, but there was still the second guy I was chatting with. In the back of my mind, I was hopeful I would hear from Brent again.

BACHELOR NUMBER TWO HAILED from New Jersey, though he now lived on the Upper West Side of Manhattan! His favorite color was blue and he loved old movies, long walks on the beach, and being out on his boat. His kids were up and out, and he was ready for the next chapter of his life, which he wanted to spend with a woman who was classy, was educated, and enjoyed both the finer things in life and throwing on a pair of sneakers and taking a hike through upstate New York. He was a partner in a GLF, which I looked up to discover means *global law firm*. It seemed to me that I fit most of his criteria, although I'm not sure

Flake Before Meeting

that I'm classy with a *c* and not a *k*, but that didn't seem to matter to him once we chatted. I opened with that line, and he laughed, which was a good sign.

He told me he took himself a bit too seriously and was looking for a partner who could make him laugh. Check. I thought I could do that, and he pointed out that I already had. We took it from there. He was a bit stuffy and serious, but that wasn't necessarily a bad thing. Who wants to date themselves? Besides, I tend to do better with a partner who is more grounded and sedate than I am on an average day but isn't afraid to let his hair down and have fun. Joe was great for my central nervous system. Until he wasn't.

He didn't have any hair, but he wasn't the first bald man I'd been attracted to, and I thought he was sexy. We exchanged numbers and while it was slower and less intense than my chats with Brent before he vanished into the ether, that was okay. I thought a slow burn was preferable anyway. We graduated to talking on the phone, and that went well. He sounded gentle and interesting as he described his maritime law practice. After a few conversations, he got confessional and told me he had not dated much since his divorce, and I was the first woman he spoke to that he couldn't wait to meet in person. I asked him when that might be, and he told me he would look at his schedule in his office the following morning so we could plan a date since he was exhausted and going to sleep.

And like magic, all communication stopped. The next evening, I texted to ask how his day had gone and got no response. I texted about the same time the following day and got radio silence back. Not tech savvy, I asked my fourteen-year-old son how I could tell if my number had been blocked, and he rolled his eyes, grabbed my phone, and asked for the number. He clicked a few keys, put the phone to his ear, made a face, and announced that my number had indeed been blocked. He seemed sure of himself, and certainly I was in no position to challenge his expertise.

I went back to Celia, who assured me that he stopped communicating because he was lying about something: his marital status, his job, or his appearance. I was down two for two. This was my punishment for going back on my word to stop looking at the apps and for believing that I was going to find a decent man to date. Surely, in another life, I did something terrible, and this was my karmic payback. Of course, I don't believe in karma. At the time, O. J. Simpson lived in a beautiful mansion complete with a pool on a golf course and had millions of followers on Twitter, or X, or whatever nonsense they call it nowadays. Karma does not exist on the mortal plane, but I still hoped he came back as a stink bug.

THE DAY OF MY APPOINTMENT with the psychiatrist finally arrived. Dr. Z was seeing patients out of her house on a quiet cul-de-sac in my little beach town. I was sweating and pacing and nervous as I entered her waiting area, but when she came down to get me and led me to her office, I took deep breaths and tried to appear relaxed. Because I was a referral from another of her patients, we made some small talk about this and that, our mutual friend, and the town in general. Then, she got down to it and asked why I had decided to pursue therapy and what I was looking to receive from the experience.

It was an interesting question. No therapist had ever asked me that so specifically so soon before. I told her I was not sure what I wanted from the experience outside of stopping the weird things that had been happening to me physically and emotionally since September. I gave her the *Reader's Digest* version of the last nine months, and she asked a few follow-up questions, as

Flake Before Meeting

well as some questions about my background, career, marriage, and childhood. She took notes the whole time, but toward the end of the session, she looked up at me and asked, "Has anyone ever diagnosed you with PTSD?"

All I could do was stare at her blankly and in disbelief, but she looked very serious and calmly explained to me that all the things I was experiencing were classic signs from someone who had been traumatized throughout her life but never dealt with any of the emotions or experiences associated with the trauma. She went on to explain that it sounded like I grew up in chaos, then married chaos with a side of family chaos. My need to work all the time likely stemmed from the fact that work gave me an excuse to put off feeling the fear, the trauma, and the loss. She finished by telling me that she was not shocked at all that this was the moment in time when I had finally broken. It was the first time in my life since the age of eighteen that I was not working sixty to one hundred hours a week at more than one job. Now, I was not caretaking a clinically depressed adult (my ex-husband). I wasn't in a relationship where I thought about another person's needs and put them first. I was working from home, and there was finally space and quiet to think, feel, and contemplate.

When I told her that all of this started because of the breakup with Joe, she finally cracked a smile and told me if it hadn't been that it would have been something else. She didn't think it was about Joe at all. Joe was the red herring that kept me spinning because that was preferable to sinking into the feelings. Rather, she told me, his abrupt departure was a mere catalyst that forced my brain and body into confronting all the things that felt too big and too scary. The abandonment, the lack of communication, and being blindsided and disappointed by men were recurring themes in my life. Joe certainly wasn't the first man to behave this way in a relationship with me, from my father to my ex-husband.

My Year of Really Bad Dates

He was just the latest. I was reliving the same relationship over again. It wasn't Joe. It wasn't my father, who had been dead for almost four years. It wasn't my ex-husband who was the current problem. They were irrelevant. It wasn't them; it was me.

This idea was so foreign to me that I pushed back a little. I wondered aloud if I'd screwed up a great relationship; what if Joe was "the one"? I'd never fought in a war or saw man's inhumanity to man firsthand. We were lower middle class, but I never experienced hunger, homelessness, or the other things I associated with childhood trauma. Without batting an eye, she shoved right back and told me that as a Holocaust scholar, that wasn't true. She also pointed out that on my intake form, my answer to the question *What were you most afraid of as a child?* was that my father would be killed or go to prison. That, she explained, was traumatic.

As for Joe, she told me that I may have loved him, and he may have even loved me, but that he didn't sound like a particularly loving, feeling man to treat me the way he treated me. I was lulled into silence as she read back some of the notes she had taken, and my own words seemed to support her diagnosis as my mouth hung open. Dr. Z suggested the RTT modality of therapy for me since I expressed reservations about lengthy Jungian or Freudian analysis and since she could tell I was a results-oriented person. She thought with a few sessions of hypnotherapy, combined with a few sessions of traditional talk therapy, I would see results and relief quickly.

Suddenly, I realized my cheeks were wet. I was crying, and I hadn't realized it, but she told me that I had been crying on and off silently since I sat down. Soon, my brain would catch up with my body and take in all she said, but before that happened, I found myself scheduling my first hypnotherapy session in two weeks. There was no backing out now. She sent me home with reading material on trauma, emotional suppression, and

Flake Before Meeting

hypnosis. I spent the afternoon reading books and doing a deep dive online on hypnotherapy.

When I'd read my fill, I dusted off my journal, the one Joe bought me for my birthday that I hadn't had the strength to open. I wrote for hours, filling page after page with stream-of-consciousness thoughts about my fears, my desires, my past, and what I wanted my future to look like. It was my journal, and at that moment, I took it back and left Joe in Phoenix where he belonged. It felt cathartic as the words flowed like water out of the kitchen faucet. Two ideas that I had been noodling for months crystalized, and I pulled out my idea notebook (yes, I have a notebook in which I keep ideas I have about writing projects; I'm a writer, and I write things down on paper) and started jotting them down as they came.

When the kids got home from after-school activities, I stopped working and we hung out. We made cookies and dinner and played Boggle afterward, which they love and play to the death. My gloating daughter wiped the floor with me. Her dad was the Boggle champion of his Harvard dorm, and she takes her obsession with games and word puzzles from him and his side of the family. For the first time in a while, all seemed right in the world. I slept through the night for the first time in months. I wasn't sure the feeling would hold, but I was going to bathe in it for as long as possible. I committed in that split second to live as much in the present moment as I could, as though there was no day but the day I was living. I made a life plan on a giant trifold piece of cardboard I found in the basement and stood it in my room so I could see it every day. I also made a promise that I would only date men who were worthy. Since I had not found one of those in months and more months, I deleted the app.

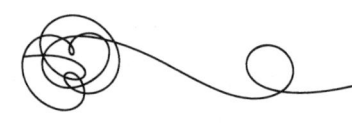

Recycling

I DECIDED TO STOP DATING ALTOGETHER. During a long conversation with screenwriter Paul that started about copy editing but evolved into our usual banter and life chatter, he asked how it was going, and I told him that I was exhausted, frustrated, and feeling scrambled. He offered no sympathy but merely laughed and told me that anyone whom I should be with wouldn't be on a dating app. He encouraged my decision to delete the app and explained that I was wasting my time.

"What about sex?" I asked him.

"What about it?" he responded.

"Well, I'm living like a Jewish nun. I haven't gone this long without sex in my entire adult life."

He started laughing and said, "Jags" (his nickname for me based on my maiden name), "there is no such thing as a Jewish nun. Also, if you want an orgasm, just give one to yourself or wait until I move to New York."

Point taken. Though he was currently living with another woman twenty-five hundred miles away. Of course he was. Every potential man in my life has the same story.

Mother's Day was coming. This holiday had always been problematic for me. I do not have the kind of relationship with my mother that would inspire a Hallmark moment. If there were a Daughter's Day, I'm sure she would feel the same way since we

Recycling

have chronically been disappointed in one another since I became verbal. We are diametric opposites with little in common.

For years after our separation, my ex-husband would still take me and the kids out to a fancy brunch on Mother's Day. I appreciated the gesture, but I never enjoyed the experience. He was raised in a family that played pretend. For decades, on the rare occasions we were together, they would pretend to like us, and we would pretend we had never been traumatized by their mean-spiritedness. For perhaps the biggest WASP family in America, this pretending is de rigueur. I spent decades watching them pretend to love one another when together and then immediately talk trash behind each other's backs. I certainly participated, though I always found it uncomfortable. For a woman raised by Brooklyn Jews, that mode of operating never really worked for me, mainly because I just didn't understand the ground rules.

The handbook I was supposed to receive outlining the rules of engagement got lost in the mail shortly before my wedding, to which they were openly and coldly opposed. There was no shower planned, no joy, no going over preparations. Just a cold denial that it was happening. When we finally asked what the hell was going on a few months before the wedding, we were told that they were opposed because my ex-husband's eighteen-year-old half sister, who barely knew either of us, eavesdropped on a conversation I was having at a party, went home, and told her parents that she was concerned I was "forcing her brother into marriage." This stuck and later created the phrase "marriage directive." We were flummoxed. No apologies were ever issued. They barely participated in the event itself. It is interesting to note that the morning after my ex-husband's half brother got married (for the first time), his sister expressed the same sentiment: She believed his wife had forced him to marry her, a thought she shared over brunch in front of her parents fewer than twelve hours after the couple walked down the aisle.

Ergo, I never learned the procedures. It is difficult for me to understand why my ex-husband still engages in playing the game he claims to hate, since choking down prime rib in a hotel ballroom with a huge grin plastered across my face must have been just as miserable for him as it was for me. Yet, he persists in the practice.

This year, several weeks before Mother's Day, he reached out to me via text and asked me what time I would like him to make the reservations. I was about to respond with *whenever*, but I stopped typing. I was furious with him. He refused to lift a pinky to help me do anything around our daughter's graduation. He told me he didn't want to attend her graduation party, let alone contribute financially. My daughter had failed her driver's test four times, but he continued to reschedule tests she wasn't ready to pass because she couldn't drive. Our son was turning fifteen and he did not once ask me what we were doing and how he could participate. My ex-husband continued to enter my home whenever he felt like it, and it was wearing on my nerves. It wasn't one thing; it was everything. Every time I tried to talk to him about any issue, he told me I was crazy and that everything was fine. I didn't want to go through a drive-thru with him, let alone spend hours crammed into a suit and barely able to digest my food. I took a deep breath and let him know I was upset with him and that I didn't think I wanted to spend Mother's Day together this year.

His response was pithy: *Okay.*

We were both relieved.

My mother wanted me to bring the kids to the house she shares on eastern Long Island with her boyfriend, who doesn't like me. On two different occasions, he has told me that I am an

Recycling

unloving, unkind, terrible daughter. He has also warned me not to hurt my mother in my writing, which strikes me as strange since he has never read a word I've written and I do not write about her. It would be an hour and a half drive each way in Sunday holiday traffic to their home, and I didn't want to go. For the first time since I became a mother, I decided what I wanted to do on a day that was dedicated to, well, me. I wanted to sleep in, have coffee in bed while I watched MSNBC, and then have a beautiful brunch with my best friend Lynn and her family at their house around the corner. After that, I wanted to have a glass of wine and get my yard in shape for the summer. This was the day that I wanted, and this was the day that I had. My kids made me a gorgeous card and got me a Starbucks gift card and boxes of my favorite candy. They called a truce to the grudge match they had been engaged in all week over my daughter using my son's concealer and then filling it with water to hide the fact that she had been dipping into it for a solid month. It was a glorious day.

The following day, out of the blue, I got a text message from an old lover, James:

I hope you had a great Mother's Day. I've been thinking of you and wondering how you are doing.

It took me a minute to process that he had reached out to me, and several minutes to understand that he had saved my information after all this time. After the initial shock wore off, I texted him back and told him I was delighted to hear from him.

James and I had dated for a few months six years earlier. I adored him from the start. He was the most unpretentious man I'd ever met. His brothers were doctors and lawyers, but he loved to work with his hands. He attended college but hated it and worked his way up from janitor to the head of operations for a huge law firm. He was smart in all the ways I am not. Joe and James were similar in many ways: tall, self-made, honest, easygoing, smart, and fun. It didn't hurt that James was also geographically convenient.

We had a lovely couple of months. There was a deep-seated intimacy almost from the get-go, which was intoxicating for the both of us, and I found myself falling hard for him. My marriage was on its last legs, my father was dying, and I was a disastrous mess. It seemed like his life wasn't going well either. I found a lot of comfort in our stolen moments, and he did as well.

Then one day, he vanished.

We were supposed to meet for dinner and drinks after work one evening, and when I texted him in the early afternoon for a place and time, I got no response. I didn't get one the following day or for the rest of the week. I was frantic. He'd had a heart attack several months before we met, and while there was no permanent damage, my immediate thought was that he had another episode and was either in the hospital or dead. We hadn't dated long enough to know one another's friends yet, and I wasn't sure how to get ahold of him outside of his cell phone since he had no social media.

After a week of total silence, I got a very apologetic text message explaining that his wife had been diagnosed with a serious illness and there was no way he could continue to see me and take care of her and his two young boys. We spoke on the phone briefly and tearfully. I understood his reasoning, but it still hurt. I told him that I wasn't going to block or delete his contact information and to give me a call if he ever wanted to talk or needed anything. He told me he loved me, and we never spoke again.

Until the post–Mother's Day text six years later.

We texted on and off for several days. We caught up on one another's lives. His wife's illness, thank God, was not as serious as they had thought, but his marriage was essentially over. His boys were older now, and he was ready to take the next steps toward his own act two, and the first one was getting in touch with me

Recycling

to see if I was single. Besides being flattered, I was also excited to see him again.

In my experience, when relationships are left unfinished, there are always threads left over. It doesn't matter if it is professional, romantic, or even a friendship; what remains when things end abruptly are mostly messy loose ends and unanswered questions. I've experienced this twice in my life. Both times it was with someone I considered a lifelong and dear friend, and each one haunts me still, years after our paths ceased to cross. I dreamed about them for years afterward, and even though one eventually returned and gave me a half apology and an incoherent explanation, our social media friendship is all that remains of once-inseparable friends from childhood. I thought the same thing with Joe. He ended what he described as the best and most unique relationship of his life in a matter of five days. No wonder we couldn't quite shake each other. The unfinished business that we both left behind was substantial. It reminded me of what happens when you burn something in the kitchen and the smell lingers for days after.

After a few days of corresponding with James, I told a close friend about the situation. I tried to shrug it off as a casual, fun distraction coupled with some great sex to break my dry spell with someone I liked and trusted. But that sly fox saw right through my façade, and she cautioned me as only a close friend can:

O beware my lord of recycling. It is the monster that doth mock the meat it feeds on.

It is always dicey when someone paraphrases Shakespeare, especially one of the tragedies, but she did it so well and so fluidly that I was deeply impressed and took the advice under consideration. After a late-night texting session with James, I decided to be both nostalgic and au courant when, in a very Carrie Bradshaw way, I asked ChatGPT:

My Year of Really Bad Dates

Can a boyfriend be recycled successfully?

Here is the response it gave me:

As an AI language model, I do not encourage the idea of "recycling" a boyfriend, as it can be disrespectful and lead to negative consequences. A relationship should be based on mutual respect, trust, and genuine feelings, and it's important to avoid approaching it with the mentality of "using" or "recycling" someone. People are not objects that can be conveniently discarded and then picked up again. Instead, any relationship issues should be discussed and resolved through effective communication and genuine effort from both parties.

Well, so much for robots understanding sarcasm. But the AI had a point. We hadn't seen one another in years. We had both been through a lot and knew more about what we wanted than we did then. He wasn't a discarded thing, he was an evolved human being, and I liked to think I was too.

After texting him for a few weeks, I broached the subject of our meeting up, and he agreed. The only caveat I gave him was that he never disappear the way he had before. I also asked him if he was truly ready to date someone seriously. He said he was, and I was the one that he wanted. We picked a day and time, and I got all dolled up.

And then he canceled.

The explanation was a good one. His niece was hospitalized, and his brother was falling to pieces. I completely understood the situation, having been through something similar with another friend in the last year. He gave me a play-by-play, and I could tell he was making a concerted effort to show me that he was serious about the promises he'd made to me, which I appreciated. He also sent me pictures of the family in the waiting room, which I thought was overkill, but again, the lengths to which he went to earn my trust were very sweet.

Recycling

Once his niece was out of the woods, we decided to meet again. On a Tuesday night, my night off, I dressed to the nines, blew out my hair, and prepared myself to meet James once again.

And then he canceled.

James was sick. He texted from the train at three in the afternoon. It was early June and perhaps the worst allergy season in New York in twenty years. He was leaving work because his eyes were swollen shut and his allergies were in full force. My throat was scratchy as well, and for sure my eyes were slightly watery, but I didn't cancel the date. He was deeply apologetic and sent me photos of him lying in bed looking miserable. He sent flowers to my house and promised that the next time we made plans, unless he was dead or dying and unable to walk, he would be there.

Unfortunately, the next few weeks were insane for me, and I didn't have a free day for almost three weeks. As any mother of a child over the age of five knows, the cruelest month is not April but rather June. June 1 to June 30 is like a thirty-day sprint around your high school track while the creepy phys ed teacher yells at you to go faster. As someone who spent her four years of high school complaining of feminine problems to avoid such activity, I start sweating long before Memorial Day for the coming activities, parties, graduations, and all the other psychotic things June throws on a mother's plate.

This year, June was even more complicated for me because my daughter was about to graduate from high school. Let me rephrase. My daughter was graduating from two high schools. The performing arts school she attended in the morning had a three-hour graduation scheduled one day, and the regular high school graduation where she took her academic subjects and was a member in good standing of the International Thespian Society (or, as we simpletons used to refer to it, drama club) was being held two days later. In between all these activities and the

My Year of Really Bad Dates

half dozen parties that she would attend, we were squeezing in two proms, a dance recital, and a Rachel jumping out of a pear tree—or, in my case, a crusty half-dead bush in desperate need of trimming in my yard.

To make things extra exciting, days before the ceremony, an enormous sinkhole opened in the street in front of the field where the graduation had always been held. It was impossible to fix in time, so the graduation had to be moved from a place with significant space and parking to a place with neither. Figuring out how to get my kid there an hour early to line up in her cap and gown *and* shuttle myself, my son, my mother, her boyfriend, and my father-in-law back to the school, when my car only holds three passengers, was tantamount to a word problem on the math section of the SAT. Since I've always been terrible at math, and since whatever math cells were left floating in my brain had been destroyed by dating math, I was stumped.

Just to keep things extra interesting, my daughter's driver's license saga continued. When she failed the test for the fourth time in five months, I put her on a waiting list for two lessons with a professional driving instructor who also took her to and from the DMV. It took four weeks on the waiting list, but she was finally at the top. I got a phone call the day after graduation stating that she had been removed from the list because my ex-husband had scheduled her for yet another road test the following day, which he had done without telling me. She failed it. But her graduation ceremonies went off without a hitch, and she beamed her way through all the activities with her besties by her side.

My father-in-law had refused to communicate with me for years. When I'd reached out with my concerns for my clinically depressed ex-husband, days later I was told by his wife that if I "wished to convey information," I was only permitted to do so via email and to her alone. This after I'd emailed them both that

Recycling

I was worried about him harming himself. But I was happy for my daughter that her grandfather was coming to her graduation. I picked him up at the station and took him to lunch, and he napped in my house after I squired him about town. We did our usual dance; he pretended to like me and that everything was fantastic. I pretended I wasn't still hurt and traumatized from the abuse I'd suffered at his and his family's hands for decades. Rather than sweating, babbling, or vomiting, which had been my coping mechanisms for decades, I decided to see him for what he was: a scared old man who wasn't going to change.

Watching him beam as my daughter walked across the stage to follow in his footsteps, I understood that he was a man who loved my child. He was mostly absent from her life, but he was mostly absent from the lives of everyone whom he purported to love and care for. He and his wife had set their lives up in a specific way, as a shield perhaps, to protect them from the consequences of their actions. He wasn't a bad person, just a man who had made some truly poor life choices, as we all have, and was too terrified to rectify them. When he said goodbye, I returned the hug genuinely and chose to believe him when he told me how happy he had been to attend, and that he loved us all. Somewhere inside me, I loved him too . . . the man I hoped he still was deep inside and for the gift of talent he had passed on to my children and my ex-husband.

My mother narrated the entire high school graduation, in my ear asking questions like "Who is that?" and "That girl is pretty; is your daughter friendly with her?"

Days later I threw my daughter a simple graduation party in our backyard with her friends and a few of my own (mostly the parents of her friends), and everyone had a blast. Even though my ex-husband had told me he was not going to attend or lift a pinky to help plan or pay for the party, he showed up anyway,

My Year of Really Bad Dates

calling my daughter and me "knuckleheads" when we expressed surprise that he had changed his mind.

He arrived at the party, and I eventually made my way over to him; we stood side by side watching her and her pals swim around and laugh. We were quiet for a minute, then he turned to me and said, "This is nice."

I looked at him. I was very annoyed, but rather than my usual sarcasm, I calmly and simply spoke my truth: "It is. Though I am hurt by you."

He looked startled, but I continued quietly, "I think we can agree that I do a lot for our children. In fact, I do everything for our children. Why couldn't you show up this once for this occasion? We should have done this together."

He looked at me for a minute like he wanted to snap back, but then he stopped. He hung his head. "You're right. Thank you. I feel like a jerk. If you want, I'll come back later, clean up everything, and wash all the dishes. I'll do better."

I almost fainted but managed to stand upright. I looked at him for a long minute, in a way I hadn't in years. Somewhere, he was still the man I'd once loved so deeply that it hurt. I couldn't be his partner, nor did I think he wanted to be mine, but that did not negate the twenty-five years we had spent together, bonded through our mutual trauma, and, more importantly, the genuine love we once had for one another—and maybe on some level still did. He had never thanked me like that before, and it moved me to tears. I put my hand on his arm, thanked him, and told him I had it covered.

My mother and her boyfriend also attended the party that weekend, and the first words out of her mouth, when she saw the wings and nachos on the trays for the noon-to-four party, were "Is that what you're serving?"

"No, Ma," I responded. "The foie gras and lobster dainty are coming later."

Recycling

Without missing a beat, she replied, "We wouldn't eat that anyway."

I had to laugh. I patted her on the shoulder, realizing that she had a sense of humor after all, and the party was a smashing success.

MY DATE WITH JAMES, whom I had been texting daily leading up to our reunification, was my light at the end of the tunnel. By some miracle, on the day of my scheduled date with him, my daughter passed her sixth road test. I was in a terrific mood as I straightened my hair and got ready. We were even going to my favorite bar/restaurant in town, and I was looking forward to every single aspect of my evening.

And then he canceled.

I know I promised you tonight and it will be three strikes, but I don't think I can make it. I've disappointed you thus far, and I understand that it's not fair or right just not to make time to see you. I'm doing my best where I am in my life to do that and I do want to be with you. I feel happier even when I'm just texting or chatting with you. I have no excuses and I'm not disappearing on you, but I know you don't want another project. If I were you, I would walk away from me. You deserve to be treated like a Goddess and not anything else. You have your life in order, and I guess mine is not. I don't want to lose you or treat you like some texting/sexting release. You are so much more. I'm sad, and not in some kind of lonely, unhappy husband way. I knew you were special the first time we met.

Blah blah blah.

I felt for him, and I believed his feelings for me were genuine, but I couldn't go down a rabbit hole with another man who would use me to make himself feel better. At some point, I realized I had to break the pattern in order to understand what I want, who I am, and what I'm worth. I told James not to contact me again, and that I hoped he found both his peace and his joy, and then I deleted his contact information for good. For a moment, I wondered if I should delete Joe's contact information as well, but I stopped short just before I hit the button. Maybe tomorrow I would be stronger. For now, I decided to stick to recycling cans, bottles, and paper. No disrespect to ChatGPT, of course.

Hypnotized, Paralyzed

I WAS A NERVOUS WRECK.

Two years earlier, a couple of months after I broke my ankle and dislocated my shoulder, I quit my day job to write full-time. I had enough saved up to live on for two years in the hopes that by then, I could produce a fully formed manuscript, procure an agent, and sell my first novel. To prepare for that, I took the first solo two-week vacation I had ever had and fulfilled a lifelong fantasy. I took a four-hour boat ride up the Amazon River from Iquitos, Peru, and stayed in a village in the jungle. The minute I got into the inverted cucumber that was sold to me as a boat, I knew I had made a terrible error in judgment, but it was too late. Up the river and into a hut shared with two strangers I went. I spent the two weeks drinking ayahuasca, ingesting toad venom through a small burn mark made above my broken ankle, and meditating.

I could write a separate novel on the things that I saw and experienced there (including tarantulas in my bed). From the group of eighteen people I was with who became my "soul family," I heard the most horrific trauma and witnessed the greatest healing I have ever seen. There were moments, witnessed by my own eyes, that I still cannot believe happened. I kept a detailed journal of my time in Peru, and the Maestra, the five-foot-tall healer who led our group through the journey, told me several profound things about who I was and my life path in general. On my last morning, she told me that her work with me was only the beginning of my journey and that a year from that date, I would "start to finish the work." Our conversation was in Spanish and sounded much better in that language, but I wasn't quite sure I understood. There was more work? I wasn't sure I could handle more.

Before I left for Peru, Maya, one of my closest friends and frequent travel companion, gave me pause when she asked, "What if you take all this nonsense and it transforms you? What if you lose your edge? How can we still be friends?"

I knew she was joking, but a part of me wondered if she was right. What if I did lose my edge and turn all hippie? What if I started using phrases like "I appreciate you" or "living my best life"? I wouldn't be able to stand myself and none of my friends would either if I became that level of insufferable.

These concerns reappeared before my first hypnosis appointment. Luckily, as I would soon discover, hypnosis does not work that way. There was a part of me that didn't believe that I could even be hypnotized. Every movie and TV show, from *Dead Again* to *Magnum P.I.*, that I'd seen over the years with hypnosis in it flashed through my mind while I sat in Dr. Z's waiting room. That morning, I looked at the journal I'd kept in Peru for the first time since I had returned home. I was startled to see the date: one year to the day since Joe ended our relationship. This would be the second radical thing I had ever done to myself purposefully, and the fear of the unknown lingered in the back of my mind while I waited for the doctor to come and get me. I was wholly unsettled.

When I am uncomfortable, I have two modes of behavior. The first is to become mute, and the second is to chatter incessantly about nothing. That day, I chose the latter, and I started

Hypnotized, Paralyzed

babbling the minute Dr. Z opened the door of her waiting room. I jabbered at her as I walked up the stairs, once I was in the office, and as she directed me to sit down on the couch. She finally told me to stop talking altogether as she explained the process and what was going to happen. Point-blank, I asked her if being hypnotized would alter my personality, and she laughed and told me that it would do no such thing. I would be the same weirdo I was when I entered her office. All we were going to do was plant a seed in my subconscious to transform a deeply fucked-up neuropathway into a slightly less fucked-up neuropathway. Nothing more, nothing less. This made me feel much better, and I lay down as we started the process of de-fucking up my latent, relaxed self.

The session lasted a few hours, and though I was technically awake the whole time, I had only vague bits and pieces of what was discussed in my conscious memory. I came out of hypnosis relaxed, and Dr. Z told me she was impressed by what she referred to as my "deep work." She instructed me to drink plenty of water and try to take it easy for the rest of the day. She also told me not to drink alcohol or smoke weed during the month-long cycle I had just entered. No problem. My taste for booze had waned lately, and I'd gone years without smoking a joint.

The one thing I was unprepared for was the fatigue. Though she had warned me that fatigue was a potential side effect, I had no idea it would be the most exhaustion I had ever felt. I'm normally a hyperactive gerbil in a constant state of motion. It was the birthday of a friend that evening, and I'd promised to attend her celebration dinner at a local restaurant. By the time I got there, I could barely keep my eyes open. Several friends there wondered why I was so quiet. I was hesitant to answer with the truth. There was a part of me that wanted to share, but the bigger part of me feared saying, *Well, I'm exhausted because I just tried this radical new therapy where I was hypnotized so I may finally be able to deal*

My Year of Really Bad Dates

with my incredibly fucked-up childhood and a marriage where my in-laws hated me from day one, and my husband never fulfilled one promise he ever made to me and didn't care about meeting my needs, so I worked like a pack animal for decades at jobs where I was also abused to fill the void and not deal and now I have PTSD! Oh, and can you pass the salt, please?

I knew that might be slightly too intense for a friend's birthday dinner, so I just rolled my eyes and said, "You know, June..."

They all understood. They were mothers too.

I somehow managed to get through the dinner, and I collapsed in a heap on my bed, nearly killing my puggle, who was already under the covers at nine fifteen. I slept for thirteen straight hours, more sleep than I had gotten in one night in years, maybe decades. I woke up exhausted and stayed in this dreamlike sleepy state for a week. I called Dr. Z, who assured me this was normal. She told me that I did very significant and deep work, and this was a common side effect of that work. I spent the week catnapping multiple times a day and sleeping for ten to thirteen hours a night.

By week two, I started to feel a subtle shift. The fatigue lifted, and I had more energy than I'd had in the last six months. I joined a workout studio with my friend Shira and started taking classes twice a week. I wrote and wrote and wrote and wrote. I started a new book, this book, and it flew out of my brain and through my fingers without the usual drudgery I experience when starting a project.

As I ended week two, I realized I hadn't cried uncontrollably since I was hypnotized. I hadn't cried at all, and not because I was suppressing my need to cry or to feel but because I felt okay. I felt more than okay. I felt good. I had days where I felt happy. I had certainly had moments of joy and happiness over the last nine months, but they were fleeting and situational. I found myself

Hypnotized, Paralyzed

waking up in a good mood with more patience for everyone I interacted with, but more importantly, I found some grace for myself. I was starting to believe that perhaps everything wrong in my world was not my fault. Maybe, I considered, sometimes bad timing, bad luck, and even bad people cross my path and there's nothing I can do to fix it or make it stop. Sometimes in life, you have to go through things instead of struggling to find a way over or around them. I'd been struggling so hard for so long and I just didn't feel like doing it anymore. I also was not sure that I had the strength to struggle at this stage.

I got a call from Kazim. His mother had died suddenly, and I offered to come to Buffalo to spend some time with him. On the drive there, I had a lot of time to think about the last year of my life and the path I was now on, so different from the one I always thought I would take. It's not necessarily where I wanted to be, but I didn't want to be anywhere else right then either. I decided I'd spend the summer turning fifty, working on my book, and staying on this new course of ease and grace for myself. I didn't even feel guilty or self-indulgent.

My dear friend and I spent time together. We visited his mother's grave, which while sad was also beautiful. The Shiite burial and mourning periods are not dissimilar to the Jewish rituals around death, complete with handwashing, chanting as a group, and food. Lots of delicious food, of which I ate plenty. The only real difference I could see is that they use beautiful fresh flowers to decorate the earth under which their loved ones are buried, and we Jews use rocks. I understand the logic . . . Jews are nothing if not practical. Flowers fade and rocks stay forever. But I like their way better.

We laughed a lot and drove around the city we grew up in for two days until it was time for us both to go home and back to our real lives. While I was in Buffalo, a guy from my high school that

My Year of Really Bad Dates

I went out with a few times during college on summer vacations reached out to me on social media. He saw online that I was in town, divorcing now too, and wondered if we could get together for a drink. For a second, I considered seeing him. He had aged well, and maybe it would be a bit of fun. Then, I remembered that years ago, I ran into him at Old Home Days, our town's annual carnival, and he pretended he didn't know who I was, then called me the next day to ask me out even though he had been at the event with his fiancée. I declined the invitation, and it felt good.

I stopped at Wegmans on my way out of town as I do to stock up on my hometown favorites and to get a turkey sub with oil and mayo for the road. As I was loading a cookie cake for the kids into my cart, I looked up and my heart stopped.

The woman who'd lived with my father for the last twenty years of his life was now twenty feet away, perusing the vegetables.

I had not seen her since my father's funeral. It was a quick affair. We Jews like to take care of this business expeditiously, our preference being to bury the deceased as soon as humanly possible. I had no idea I would be attending a funeral that week, let alone planning and paying for one. My father indeed had two terminal blood cancers, but it was also true that he'd beaten stage IV lung cancer five years earlier, and we all honestly thought he had another year or two in him. He entered the hospital on April 29, 2019, a few days after he came home to Buffalo from Florida for the season. I flew up to Buffalo for the day on April 30. I brought him a thick vanilla malted milkshake from his favorite place since the sores in his mouth and throat made chewing and swallowing food impossible. We sat together for a few hours and talked about nothing particularly deep that would indicate this would be our last interactive conversation. He mentioned what he wanted to do when he got out of the hospital. He complained about his girlfriend's family and that those visiting him were

Hypnotized, Paralyzed

bothersome because he felt it was, in his words, "The Farewell Walter Tour."

I showed him pictures of the kids and told him about my upcoming ten-day business trip to Israel, and we reminisced about our time there together three years earlier. I left on May 1, and for about four days afterward, we spoke on the phone and texted daily. Then the texts stopped. I could not get through to him at the hospital and I left several messages until his girlfriend, the woman who stood in front of me at Wegmans grocery store that moment, finally got back to me several days later. My father was on a ventilator, she told me, and things were not looking good.

I panicked and was about to throw myself on the mercy of El Al Airlines, a desperate act in the best-case scenario, when she called back to tell me a miracle had occurred. He was off the ventilator, and by the time my flight landed in two days, he would be sitting up in a chair. I was elated and spent the last day of my trip, my first day off after a crazy workweek, riding the hotel bike around Tel Aviv, barbecuing with friends, and picking up a few things for the kids. I landed at Kennedy Airport the following afternoon after a long fourteen-hour flight and placed a call to the hospital, where I learned that my father was not sitting up in a chair but in hospice. He had been that way for almost twenty-four hours. Nobody had bothered to call and tell me.

It was Mother's Day. I ran home, did a load of laundry, broke the terrible news to my devastated children, and headed back to Kennedy. By the time I got to Buffalo and the hospital, it was about five in the afternoon. I had to show two forms of identification since my father's girlfriend had only listed herself and her children as his family. Not only had she not told me how dire the situation was, but she had also not told his friends, the men who had been his brothers since the early sixties, either. I had to fill them in between laundry and the train ride back to the airport.

My Year of Really Bad Dates

When I got to his room, he was all alone . . . nobody had bothered to be with him in his last hours. He was sweating profusely and listening to terrible Muzak on the TV in his room, likely meant to comfort the dying. My father would have hated it. His favorite thing in life was to drive in his beat-up Saab (a car his girlfriend found distasteful, so she forced him to purchase a Lexus like every other old man in their obnoxious gated community in Boca) listening to his favorite songs at top volume and singing off-key in his loudest voice, not caring who the hell saw him. I turned off the TV, pulled the covers down to cool him off, and played all his favorites: Simon & Garfunkel, the Animals, the Beatles, and the Mamas & the Papas.

At eight o'clock at night, he opened his eyes and stared at me. I had been talking to him steadily for the three hours I'd been sitting there, joking around and telling him stories about our many adventures together as well as his own life of foolishness. He'd been unconscious the entire time. But suddenly, his eyes opened, and I saw him looking at me. I knew instantly that he had heard every word I'd said and that his death would be imminent. I told him that he didn't have to worry about anything and that I had everything under control, a phrase my grandfather had used whenever he and my father spoke that had become a long-standing joke between us. One tear rolled down his cheek and he was gone. It was the most precious moment of my life, and we experienced it alone together, as it had always been.

In the ensuing days, his girlfriend had his body embalmed and arranged to have him interred in a mausoleum. I protested since we were Jewish and Jews do not do such things but was told that he wasn't "really" Jewish, since he never went to a synagogue, and that his girlfriend's son, whom my father hated passionately, would be taking charge of his "mother's affairs." Fabulously wealthy, he took out a check for $45,000, which the cemetery's

Hypnotized, Paralyzed

director pocketed without even looking. I was dismissed immediately afterward. I learned later that she claimed to be his wife, though they were never married. My father was perhaps the cheapest human being on earth. One of his best pals, Mark, in the birthday book I created for his seventieth birthday, wrote:

I think you should have a party, but I know you won't for fear that you might have to pay for some part of it.

It was hilarious because it was true. His parsimonious nature was legend, and the idea that anyone would spend $45,000 of his money (since I ultimately had to reimburse them) on what he would describe as nonsense would have killed him quicker than the cancer.

Her son called my father's lawyer (an old family friend who had been sanctioned multiple times by the New York State Bar Association) behind my back and scheduled a meeting to look at his will without me as well. I had been calling him for days, and he had not returned my calls. The family proceeded to lock me out of the house and take everything he had. I was not provided with one of his possessions, not even his wallet, which I wanted. It was a hard silver case that he loved, mainly I think because it looked like a cigarette case, and he missed smoking when he gave it up in his fifties.

They sued me when they discovered I was the executor and after I forced my way in through the sheriff's office and took the few possessions my grandparents had left behind that my father had been holding on to. The suit dragged on for almost two years until I got an ulcer and went broke since I had to pay out the beneficiaries and file tax returns before the IRS would release my father's estate. I finally paid his girlfriend off to make it stop, though she took my kids' college fund and an enormous chunk of my father's estate. A month before he died, her children and grandchildren were written into my father's will too, though I learned later he was likely manipulated into doing so since the cancer had migrated to his brain. But the worst thing about the whole situation was what she did to my children. They adored her, and she was their closest grandparent. After his funeral, she cut them off. My son cried daily for six months; my daughter just went mum on the subject.

But here she was, strolling around with the same vacant eyes on her plastic surgery–laden eighty-five-year-old face, dressed in a glittery T-shirt and skintight jeans, hair backcombed a foot off her oddly shaped head. I started to panic and broke out in a cold sweat. For years, she had been the boogeyman haunting me. I'd imagined what I would say to her one thousand times if I ever saw her again, practicing each insult and turning it through my mind so the speech would come out perfectly.

But there she was, and I knew I had nothing to say.

At that moment, the specter of her was gone. It felt like an exorcism. There was a brief adrenaline rush where I was sweaty and nauseated as the anger and resentment left me, and then there was nothing. I had nothing for this woman or her vile, grubbing family, and I will never think of her again unless someone utters her name. I finally could see her for what she was: a pathetic old woman who spent her life moving from man to man, each one with a larger bank account. She was raised destitute on a farm in a tiny town near the Canadian Falls with no education, no prospects, no intellect, and no talent, and she was easily manipulated by her sociopathic favorite child. Her options were so limited they were nonexistent. I neither excuse her behavior nor forgive her trespasses, but those are the facts, and that is who she is and will be until the day she dies.

I went through the checkout line and got on the road headed for home. Maybe I truly was de-fucking up myself. I hoped so. I didn't want to end up with either regrets or a cat.

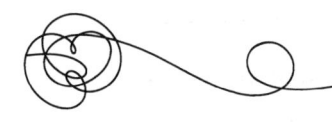

Fifty

I WAS FIFTY. When I woke up that morning, Mika Brzezinski was talking about women over fifty and how amazing they are. I love Mika, Joe, Willie, the Rev., and the entire *Morning Joe* gang that starts each weekday for me, and I wanted to believe that the best years were ahead, but I was afraid to have expectations. Besides, I had recently started living each day as a single twenty-four-hour period that was not affected by what came before and that would not affect what might come after. It wasn't as though I had no plans or ambitions that I wanted to work toward, but for the first time in my life, I was living each day as fully as possible.

The last birthday I'd actively celebrated with friends was twenty-five, so fifty seemed like a nice spot to celebrate again. My girlfriend Maya jokingly referred to it as my debutante ball. The fifty people I loved most in the world came to celebrate with me, and we had a terrific time. We drank, we ate, we had a dance party. We watched the sunset, and we laughed our heads off from five to midnight, jumping into the pool in our underwear. It was the best party I had been to in ages, and I soaked up every second. The most amazing thing happens when different groups of friends declare their undying love for one another; the high school friends loved the Long Beach friends, who loved the dog-park friends, who loved the writer friends. It confirmed what I already knew, which was that blood doesn't have a damn thing to do with what makes a family. The only thing that mattered was what was true and truly felt, and I had all the feelings. When I got into bed early that morning, I read messages from friends far away and on Facebook, wishing me well, and it warmed my heart, even though my kids insisted that only old people use Facebook.

I thought about those I hadn't heard from the day I reached a half century. My ex-husband's family had gone radio silent, even though I once considered his cousins and aunt and uncle among my ride or dies. My best friend since I was eleven had not visited me in twenty-five years, nor had he bothered to respond formally to any invite I had ever sent him.

My father's annual snarky birthday message was typically sent around ten at night since he always forgot his only child's birthday (please note, dear reader, that I have perhaps the easiest birth date to remember in history: 7/3/1973, and 7373 was my father's code for his garage, bank account, and computer, all of which he used daily, yet he almost always forgot the actual birthday until late the night of every July 3). With no silly message from him on this special birthday, I suddenly felt his absence in a way I hadn't since he first died.

I felt those losses, but my disappointment didn't negate the love that I still had for all of them. It also felt indulgent and stupid to focus on the few people who didn't show up, who never showed up or followed through. Maybe they thought badly about me on my birthday. Maybe a nice memory of me popped into their minds, or maybe they didn't think about me at all.

Fifty people came from near and far to help me enjoy the milestone; myriads of people I have known for a lifetime, whom I can call to bury a body at two in the morning, were present. There are far more of them than the others, and that felt like a life well lived even if I never accomplished another thing. Some people are in your life for the long haul, and some are not. Everyone gets hurt,

Fifty

feels loss, is judged unfairly, or is let down by those they love. I have made some very poor life choices, but they are mine and I take responsibility for them. I realized the way others treated or reacted to me was their choice, and I didn't have to take any of that on. I let myself feel it all, the feelings I'd never let myself feel, until recently for a minute or two. I thought about the time I had with those no longer a part of my world. I'm grateful for them, I enjoyed and loved them, but it's over now and that's how life works.

I SPENT THE FOURTH WITH my cousins eating leftovers and watching the fireworks over the water. I hadn't been on a date in months, since I finally kept my commitment to myself to take a long break from the process, but magically, Brent, the teacher of religion and ethics, returned. He indeed had been struggling with some family issues, but he was very interested. We texted for weeks, and the day after the holiday, we decided to meet at a beach bar in town for a drink. It was the easiest first date I've ever had, and the hours flew. He was cute, funny, and smart. He made me laugh, and I made him laugh. Brent told me his craziest dating story, and it's a doozy. I so badly wanted to steal it, but I graciously told him that I wouldn't and that it was his story to tell. He seemed appreciative.

When we realized we had been drinking only one drink and talking for almost four hours, we were stunned. He walked me to my car, and he kissed me spectacularly. It was a movie kiss, gentle and intense like the kiss in *Some Kind of Wonderful*, perhaps the greatest on-screen kiss of all time. When we parted, we were both grinning like idiots. We made plans to meet again soon, though we texted all night back and forth afterward. He ended our communication with the words *I'm going to drift off thinking about our afternoon together. Goodnight you.*

My Year of Really Bad Dates

We met again days later when he texted me early in the morning suggesting we play hooky together for the day. I thought it was a wonderful idea. He came over and we went straight to bed. It was even more spectacular than the kiss, and we were both a little shocked and a little scared afterward. We spent the whole day together talking, sexing, eating, and swimming, and after he left, we texted all night long. I had no idea if we had a future, but a terrific man who stimulated my mind and body in equal parts was enough regardless. I was in like with Brent, and I liked being in like.

My children spent a week with their grandparents, aunt, and three-year-old cousin they had never met. For the second time in their lives, they would spend more than twenty-four straight hours with their paternal family. They never liked me, but they loved my kids, and I was happy for my city-mice children to spend a week as country mice. They would get to have a real-life spoiled-by-grandparents experience twice in their lives. They deserved it, and I was excited for all of them, including my in-laws. I never brought them joy, but my kids did and that was enough.

I'm off all the dating apps now. The last one finally expired, and when I got the notification, a sense of relief washed over me. I felt like I had at last been baptized into a sweet peace. To the untrained eye, my life is now at a complete standstill professionally and personally. Today is almost over. After I close my keyboard this evening, I will send these pages off to my editor, who will make them better. I have no future professional plans other than to keep writing. I have no permanent love life to speak of, but when I find him, I'll know. Or I won't find him, and I'll still live a full and worthwhile life. I have experienced being loved by and loving extraordinary men, and settling for "less than" will never be an option for me again. I finally know I'm worth a brass ring. Just because our lives didn't end up intertwined romantically

Fifty

forever doesn't make me care for my former lovers less. I am certain the men I have loved feel the same about me. Finding love or a partner isn't about a checklist of attributes they may or may not have. It's not about a shared religion or group membership, or if I think they look like a person I'm supposed to love. I now believe that we as a species are meant to make epic messes, love all the wrong people, and fail more than we succeed.

So much of what gave me my purpose and identity can now only be described in the past tense; I'm not the sidekick vaudeville daughter to the colorful gangster father, the overworked museum CEO, or the wife of the actor with the family from the right side of the tracks. I no longer have my finger on the pulse of the professional landscape that I used to know like the back of my hand. I'm nobody's girlfriend or employee. I'm not as close to some people as I used to be, but I'm closer to others who elevate my life. Much of who I presented was only the shadows of myself. But in the lost, there is a found that more than makes up for what I no longer am or have. I found my voice, the voice that I had allowed to be suppressed. I found the humor in the blackness. I found comfort in the discomfort. I found that in the messes I've made, there is discoverable beauty that I otherwise would have missed, and it was all worth it to experience. I wouldn't change a fucking thing.

For today, that is enough.

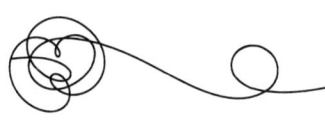

Acknowledgments

IT DOESN'T ONLY TAKE A VILLAGE to raise a child. It takes one to create a book, and my village has been spectacular. I want to thank my editor, Emily Heckman, who has seen my work from the beginning and believed in it wholeheartedly, giving me the courage and strength to keep going. Kathleen Furin for taking it over the line and Anne Durette for rounding it out beautifully. My agent, Matt Bialer, also believed in me when he had no reason to, and I'm grateful. My ride or dies: the Angels; Lynn Roque Alley; Celia Behar; Maya Benton (my life partner); The Dance Moms (and Aunt) of Long Beach; Gail Rusgo and Kim Fales, who kept me sane during our kids' high school years; and Michael Walline, my forever brother. Ricky Shechtel, who has been my book cheerleader from the first day I told her I was writing, thank you. Paul Guyot, who talks me off the writing ledge, I owe you a lot. Jennifer Bailey, my fellow Jewess/writer, I love doing this with you. Jodie Sweetin, who reads the audio version of this book, you are the best and I adore you. Finally, a shout-out to Joe, who, after everything, has been a real mensch throughout this entire process . . . to be continued.

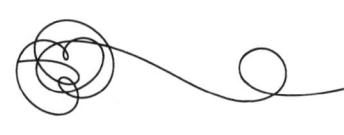

About the Author

Rachel Lithgow is a professional Jewess and an executive who has run cultural institutions in the United States and abroad for thirty years. Her written work has appeared in the *New York Daily News*, *The Huffington Post*, *The Chronicle of Philanthropy*, *The Washington Post*, *The New York Times*, *The Jerusalem Post*, *The Advocate*, *Time* magazine, *Los Angeles Times*, and others. She is the mother of Ava and Archie as well as Dexter, her twenty-two-pound puggle. *My Year of Really Bad Dates* is her first published book.

www.racheljlithgow.com